The Artistic Splendor of the Spanish Kingdoms:

The Art of Fifteenth-Century Spain

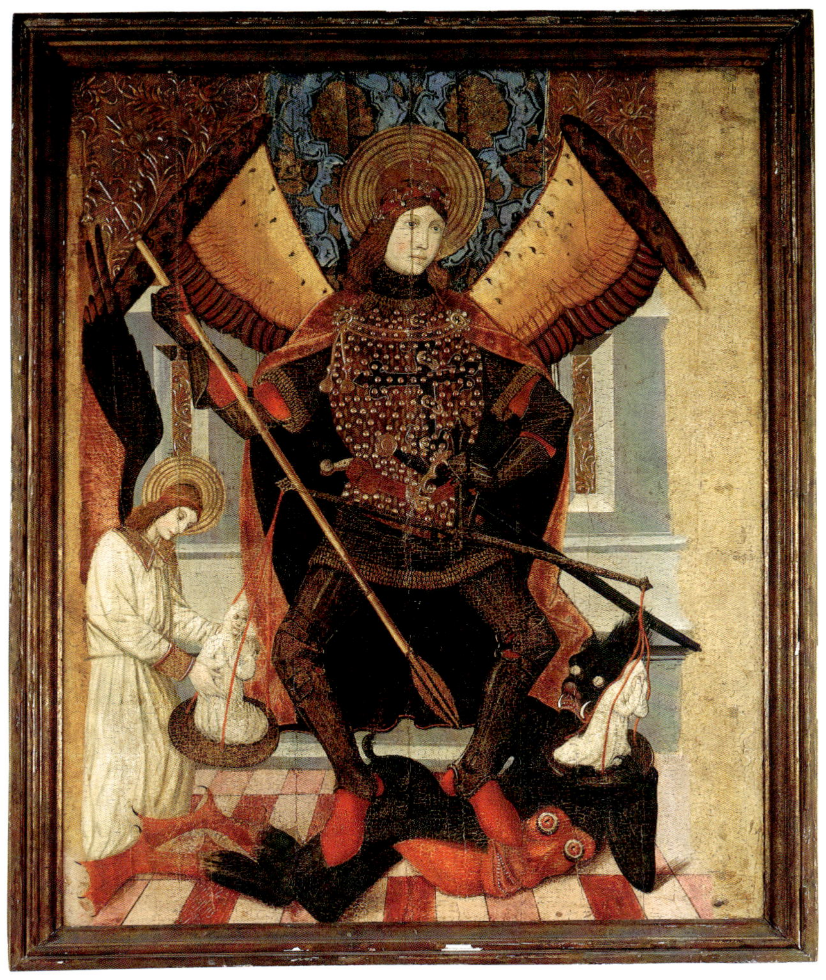

Pere García de Benabarre, *St. Michael*, after 1461

This catalogue is published to accompany the exhibition organized by the Isabella Stewart Gardner Museum.

The exhibition and catalogue are made possible in part by a grant from the National Endowment for the Arts, a Federal agency.

"The Artistic Splendor of the Spanish Kingdoms: The Art of Fifteenth-Century Spain"
Isabella Stewart Gardner Museum, Boston
January 13–April 7, 1996

Cover: *Saint Engracia* (detail) by Bartolomé Bermejo
Isabella Stewart Gardner Museum, Boston. See Cat. No. 1a.
Photo by David Bohl, 1995.

Frontispiece: St. Augustine of Hippo,
De Civitate Dei ("On the City of God")
© The Metropolitan Museum of Art, New York.
See Cat. No. 15.

Published by the Trustees of the
Isabella Stewart Gardner Museum
Two Palace Road, Boston, Massachusetts 02115

Photograph credits appear on pages 62–63.

ISBN 0-9648475-1-5

The Artistic Splendor of the Spanish Kingdoms: The Art of Fifteenth-Century Spain

Judith Berg Sobré
Lynette M. F. Bosch

Isabella Stewart Gardner Museum

Boston, Massachusetts

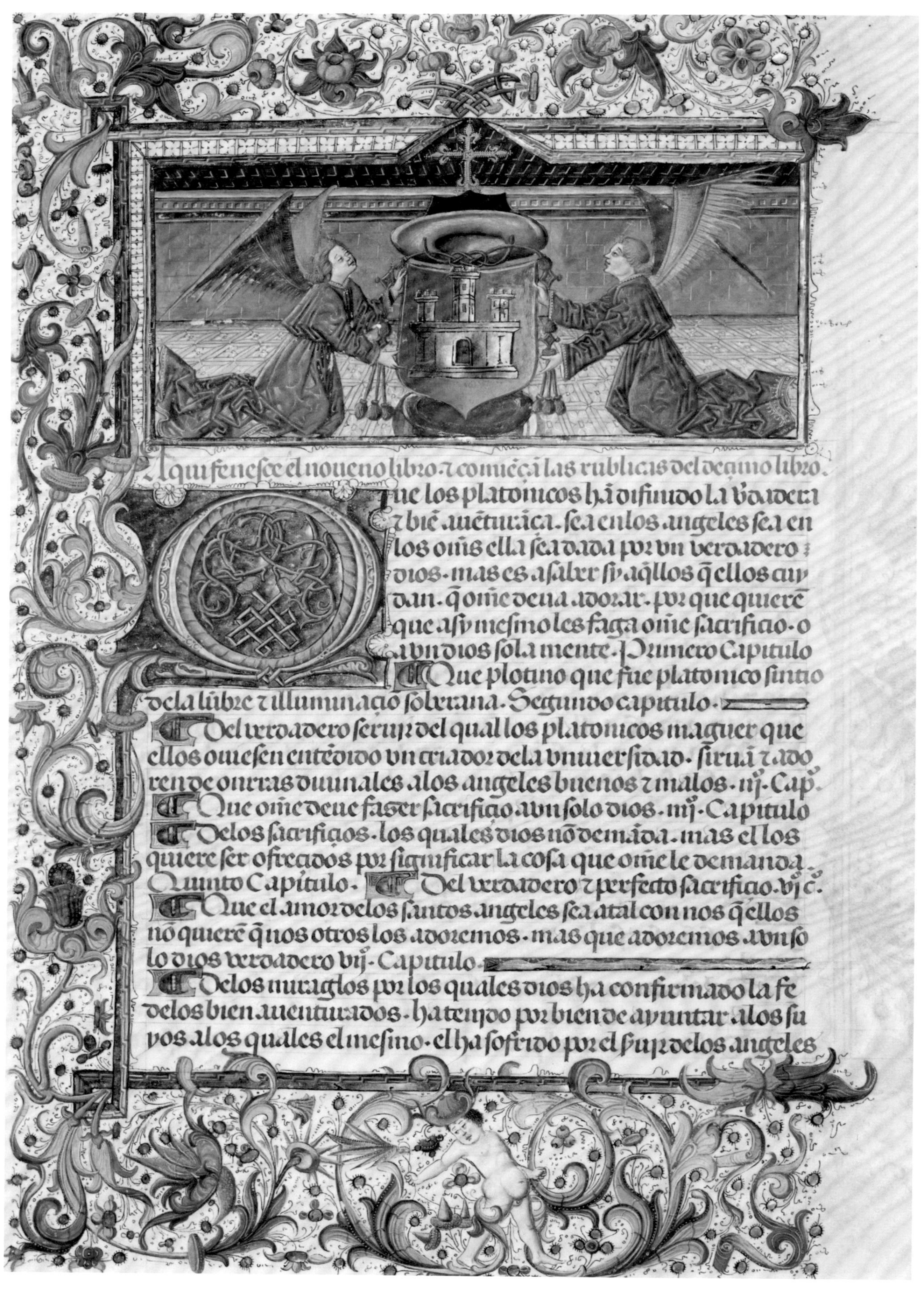

Aqui fenesçe el noueno libro ⁊ comieçã las rublicas del deçimo libro.

Que los platonicos hã difinido la v̄dera ⁊ biẽ auẽturãça. sea enlos angeles sea en los omñs ella sea dada por vn verdadero dios. mas es a saber si aq̃llos q̃ ellos au dan. q̃ ome deua adorar. por que quierẽ que asy mesmo les faga ome sacrifiçio. o a vn dios sola mente. Primero Capitulo

¶ Que plotino que fue platonico sintio dela lũbre ⁊ illuminaçio soberana. Segundo capitulo.

¶ Del verdadero seruiçio del qual los platonicos maguer que ellos ouiesen entẽdido vn criador dela vniuersidad. siruiã ⁊ adoraron de onrras diuinales alos angeles buenos ⁊ malos. iijº. Cap.

¶ Que ome deue faser sacrifiçio a vn solo dios. iiijº. Capitulo

¶ Delos sacrifiçios. los quales dios nõ demãda. mas el los quiere ser ofreçidos por significar la cosa que ome le demanda. Quinto Capitulo.

¶ Del verdadero ⁊ perfecto sacrifiçio. vjº c.

¶ Que el amor delos santos angeles sea atal con nos q̃ ellos nõ quierẽ q̃ nos otros los adoremos. mas que adoremos a vn solo dios verdadero vijº. Capitulo.

¶ Delos miraglos por los quales dios ha confirmado la fe delos bien auenturados. ha tenido por bien de ayuntar alos suyos alos quales el mesmo. el ha sofrido por el seruiçio delos angeles

CONTENTS

LENDERS TO THE EXHIBITION

P & D Colnaghi
London and New York

Davis Museum and Cultural Center, Wellesley College
Wellesley, Massachusetts

Harvard University Art Museums
Cambridge, Massachusetts

Isabella Stewart Gardner Museum
Boston, Massachusetts

Museum of Art, Rhode Island School of Design
Providence, Rhode Island

San Diego Museum of Art
San Diego, California

The Houghton Library, Harvard University
Cambridge, Massachusetts

The Metropolitan Museum of Art
New York, New York

The Minneapolis Institute of Arts
Minneapolis, Minnesota

The Pierpont Morgan Library
New York, New York

The Textile Museum
Washington, D.C.

Williams College Museum of Art
Williamstown, Massachusetts

PREFACE

Over the last four years, the Gardner Museum has mounted a series of exhibitions, directed on parallel paths: those focusing new perspectives on works of visual and cultural interest within the collection and those providing a showcase for works by contemporary artists inspired by the collection and its unique setting.

In 1996, we have the opportunity to explore one of the little-known strengths of our collection, the art of fifteenth-century Spain. This exhibition, "The Artistic Splendor of the Spanish Kingdoms: The Art of Fifteenth-Century Spain," is particularly welcome as, remarkably, it is the first such show in this country. Organized by the Gardner's chief curator of collections, Dr. Hilliard Goldfarb, and the leading American expert in the field, Dr. Judith Berg Sobré, of the University of Texas at San Antonio, the exhibition and catalogue redefine public perception of the period.

As Dr. Sobré's introductory essay to this catalogue notes, the fifteenth century is generally viewed as one of provincialism in which the Spanish kingdoms adopted foreign stylistic currents. In this reinterpretation, it is revealed as a century of vibrant, diverse cultures on the Iberian Peninsula, absorbing and reinterpreting influences as diverse as Flemish painting and Islamic design. Paintings, sculptures, textile, and manuscripts have been selected to better understand these regional styles and cultures. Dr. Lynette M.F. Bosch, of Brandeis University, generously assisted in the selection of manuscripts, Catholic and Jewish, for the exhibition and wrote the catalogue entries for those texts.

We are profoundly grateful to the many museums and libraries across the country who, recognizing its historic nature, have participated in this exhibition with us.

We also extend our gratitude to the National Endowment for the Arts, whose partial support enabled this project to move forward. Within the institution itself, special thanks are extended to Jill Medvedow, deputy director for programming, for oversight of the project; Patrick McMahon, registrar; and Kären Croff Bates, curator of education, who oversaw the development and coordination of the exciting outreach and educational programs associated with the exhibition.

Cultural interchange and the relationships of minority cultures within a broader society are at the heart of this project. It is our hope that this exhibition will give visitors a sense of the rich, now vanished cultures which flourished during the fifteenth century in what is now a unified Spain: the distinctly differing Christian cultures of the Crown of Aragon and the Kingdom of Castile, and the cultural interchange that existed between the Iberian Peninsula's three religious groups—Muslims, Jews, and Christians.

Anne Hawley, *Director*
Isabella Stewart Gardner Museum

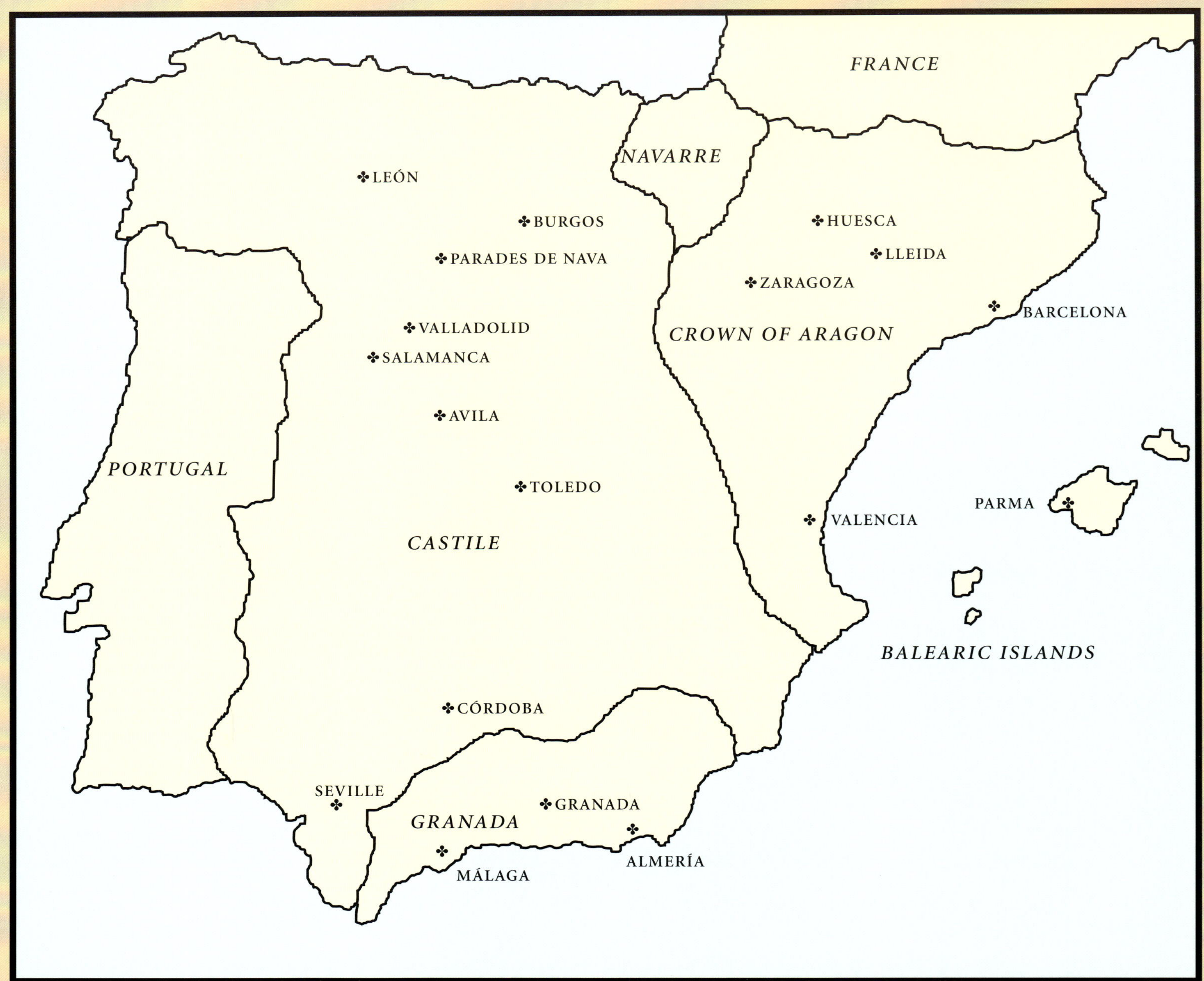
FRANCE
NAVARRE
LEÓN
BURGOS
PARADES DE NAVA
HUESCA
LLEIDA
ZARAGOZA
BARCELONA
CROWN OF ARAGON
VALLADOLID
SALAMANCA
AVILA
PORTUGAL
TOLEDO
PARMA
VALENCIA
CASTILE
BALEARIC ISLANDS
CÓRDOBA
SEVILLE
GRANADA
GRANADA
ALMERÍA
MÁLAGA

Figure 1

THE ARTISTIC CLIMATES OF LATE MEDIEVAL SPAIN

The fifteenth century was an historical watershed for Spain, for it brought the end of a seven-hundred-year-long Holy War and with it a medieval philosophical outlook. It therefore marked the gateway to Spain's role as a totally Catholic and world power. The visual arts experienced a corresponding shift (though with a slight time lag) that was directly affected by political, religious, and social change and which permeated all corners of production.

The political map of the Iberian Peninsula in 1400 (fig. 1) looked much as it did in 1250, shortly after the Christians conquered Seville and effectively put the Reconquest on hold. There were, at the beginning of the fifteenth century, five separate realms on the Iberian Peninsula. Portugal occupied a strip in the southwest extending north to the Miño river, where it bordered on Galicia. Castile made up more than half the total area of the Iberian Peninsula, extending from Galicia in the northwest south to the Atlantic, east of Portugal nearly to the Straits of Gibraltar, east from there to a short segment of coastline along the Mediterranean, then north and slightly west to the Cantabrian Sea. Included within Castile were the former kingdoms of León, Galicia, and Asturias (the seminal point for the Reconquest seven hundred years earlier); a portion of Basque lands; and a sizeable chunk of what was once Al-Andalus, including Córdoba, once the seat of the Muslim Caliphate, and the ancient Visigothic capitals of Seville and Toledo, which had in turn been important Islamic cities.[1]

To the north and east was the Crown of Aragon, which was subdivided into smaller realms: Catalonia with its capital, Barcelona, to the northeast; Aragon, the only completely inland section to Catalonia's west; Valencia, a roughly triangular territory, to the south; and the Balearic Islands in the Mediterranean Sea.[2] The smallest Christian Kingdom was Navarre, located between Aragon and Castile in the north. The majority of Navarre's population was of Basque descent, but it was ruled by descendents of the counts of Champagne, with considerable injections from both the Aragonese and Castilian ruling lines through marriage. Finally, there was the Kingdom of Granada, the last remnant of Muslim rule on the peninsula. Consisting of a relatively modest strip along the Mediterranean, it encompassed the cities of Granada, Málaga, and Almería.

The character of each of these kingdoms was very different. Leaving aside Portugal and Navarre, which will not figure in this exhibition, and which were not united by fifteenth-century political and military moves of the Catholic Kings, a look at the remaining three kingdoms will set the stage for an examination of the artistic developments within them.[3]

The Crown of Aragon had been the great commercial power on the Iberian Peninsula during the thirteenth and fourteenth centuries, chiefly through the great port and manufacturing center of Barcelona, in Catalonia. Catalan merchants had shipped woolens and other goods of local manufacture from the region and the Aragonese interior to many Mediterranean ports in exchange for diverse import goods. At the same time, there had been a strong local banking industry. These enterprises had encouraged the rise of a strong middle class, and some families had made so much profit that they lived and ruled as wealthy aristocrats (under the deceptively modest name of *ciutadans honrats*, honored citizens). There was also a substantial artisan class, which prospered in the fat years, even though the artisans had little political power. Barcelona's hegemony began to slip after the arrival of the Black Death in 1348. Its outbreak and subsequent recurrences caused severe depopulation (in Barcelona alone, nearly half the inhabitants died) and a consequent decline in Catalan agriculture. The later collapse of local banks in the face of Genoese expansion further contributed to Barcelona's decline.

The economy and position of Valencia was somewhat different. To begin with, its agricultural base was broader and it had a large population of resident Muslims (Mudéjars) who were farmers. Rice, oranges, and other crops were grown in the fertile soil of the area not only for local consumption but also for export. Mudéjar artisans likewise dominated the ceramics industry, which also commanded an export market. The city of Valencia itself was becoming an important commercial center, exporting fine brocades and silks, as well as leather goods and furniture, in exchange for European and Near Eastern luxury goods.

The Balearic Islands, strategically located in the Mediterranean, was a crossroads for trade among Provence, Italy, and the Iberian Peninsula. Within the Crown of Aragon, Aragon itself occupied a unique position. Totally land-locked, its economy was dependent on sheep and their byproducts (wool and leather goods), as well as on farming. Its culture was more insular than that of its coastal neighbors, its middle class smaller, the power of its feudal nobles somewhat greater. In some ways, Aragon's social and economic situation was closer to that of Castile.

Castile, too, lacked manufacturing, and its economy was also largely wool-based—to the point that most mercantile activity was centered around wool and its products. Trade generally flourished around great inland towns (such as Medina del Campo, the site of a regional fair, or Burgos, a town on a main travel route to Northern Europe, Castile's principal market area) instead of in maritime trading cities. In general, however, the Castilian merchant class was very small, and the artisan class was nowhere near the size of its counterpart in Catalonia,Valencia, and the Balearic Islands.

Whereas the Crown of Aragon, and particularly Catalonia, had a well-developed feudal system (legacy of an early Carolingian alliance), Castile, being long in the thick of Reconquest activity, had developed a looser relationship between king and nobles. Many of the nobility had been granted titles, privileges, and land in exchange for fighting in recently acquired territories that needed to be repopulated as the Reconquest progressed. Some of these noble families became extremely powerful as they increased their land holdings, but a far greater number became more and more impoverished. Part of this impoverishment was also due to a disdain for manual labor among members of the noble class, even among those who were land-poor; the case of a painter such as Pedro Berruguete coming from this noble class is an outstanding exception.

A great deal of Castile's land was too poor to farm; instead, the land was given over to great herds of migrating sheep. The more fertile soil of Andalusia supported not only agriculture, but large cattle ranches, which were usually owned by a few great aristocratic families. Cattle were raised both for meat and for hides. Indeed, the cowboys and *vaqueros* of the Americas had their roots in medieval Andalusia. As in Aragon, Andalusia sustained a sizeable Mudéjar farming population.

Although governmental and economic systems in the Kingdom of Castile and the Crown of Aragon differed in many ways, they were similar in being ruled by Catholic dynasties that generally allowed Muslims and Jews to live in their lands on suffrance. The conditions of their residence within the Catholic Kingdoms included, at different periods, the paying of stiff taxes, the wearing of certain prescribed garments, and the stipulation that their religious buildings be less conspicuous than their Christian counterparts or that no new ones be built at all.

For Muslims, at least, the situation was quite different in the Kingdom of Granada. The ruling Nasrid dynasty was founded by Muhammed I of Arjona (Ibn al-Ahmar) in 1242, and that dynasty continued in power until the fall of Granada in 1492. The land ruled by the Nasrids was a mere remnant of the great territories that made up Al-Andalus during the first five hundred years of the Islamic presence in the Iberian Peninsula. As the thirteenth century progressed, pressure to whittle down the kingdom even more came from Christian armies on all sides of Granada. To secure their position, the Sultans of Granada declared themselves vassals of the Kings of Castile in 1243. Most of the time, this state of vassalage was an uneasy one, and for greater security, the Nasrid rulers also made an alliance with the Marinid dynasty of the Maghrib in North Africa. For these reasons, the Nasrids' posture was by necessity a defensive one, and it is not surprising that their culture turned inward, centering on their capital, Granada, and the opulent palace of the Alhambra, whose lengthy building campaigns under a succession of fourteenth-century rulers are generally viewed as a gorgeous political statement of a waning monarchy's apparent, if not actual, power.

A great deal of political activity in medieval Spain was domestic, centering on the consolidation of power and territory within the peninsula by its often warring monarchs. (The most significant exception was Catalonia's expansionist policy in the Mediterranean, which led it to conquer Sicily in 1282, encompass Sardinia and Corsica, and even including the occupation of Athens in 1311 by Catalan and Aragonese mercenaries.) But in the fifteenth century, the situation began to change.

Two events involving conflicts between Christianity and Islam—one within the Iberian Peninsula, the other on the other side of the Mediterranean—were to have consequences that would bring about radical change. The earlier of the two was the Turkish conquest of Byzantine Constantinople in 1453. With the Turks dominating the eastern Mediterranean, easy trade with the Middle East and Orient was no longer possible, for the Christians no longer had the relatively friendly link with the East that they had enjoyed with Byzantium. At the same time, the Mediterranean itself became more dangerous, for the number of North African and Ottoman pirates increased. All of these changes led the Portuguese to explore alternate routes to Far Eastern trade, first down the African coast and then around Cape Horn to India. And it ultimately led to the westward voyages of Columbus.

The second event was the conquest of Granada, begun under the Catholic Kings in 1484 and completed eight years later. As we have seen, the Kingdom of Granada occupied only a very small portion of the Iberian Peninsula, and its conquest seems to have been put off until this time not because of any Muslim military strength, but because of other demands on Castile and the Crown of Aragon. At any rate, the final Christian triumph over the last vestiges of Islamic occupation in the Iberian Peninsula was a victory with tremendous psychological implications for both the rulers and citizens of Christian Spain. Once victory was achieved, the Christians no longer needed to be so tolerant, and so the religious minorities in the Iberian Kingdoms became increasingly marginalized, and finally were expelled.

The first to go were the Jews. The sometimes easy, sometimes uneasy coexistence of the peninsula's Jews and Christians was by 1400 rapidly becoming a thing of the past. By that time, the Jews had lost much of their presence. Their population had already been decimated by the pogroms of 1391, which occurred both in Castile and in Aragon. Many Jews were killed at that time, while an even larger number became converts; some cities like Barcelona and Córdoba lost their entire Jewish populations.[4] The conversions were by and large unforced, for there is evidence that much of the spiritual vitality of the Jewish communities in many places had been eroding for some time. Thus the events of 1391 and subsequent campaigns to convert Jews, particularly in Aragon (including the preachings of the Dominican friar Vicent Ferrer and the Jewish-Christian debates at Tortosa from 1413 to 1414, convened by the Anti-Pope Benedict XIII), apparently met with a great deal of success.[5] There were, of course, Jews who remained true to their faith, and they continued to prosper in Castile during the fifteenth century, but it was the Catholic Kings' belief that these Jews would put pressure on the converts to revert to Judaism that caused their expulsion in 1492. However, life for the converts proved even more difficult as the century wore on. Though some rose to high positions within the Kingdom of Castile and within the Church, the faith of many was suspect, and many would eventually fall victim to the Inquisition, which was designed to root out heresies within Castile and Aragon.

For the Catholic Kings, and for Spain's subsequent history, the expulsion of the Jews would prove to be a disaster. Among the 150,000 to 300,000 Jews who left the country were some of the greatest commercial minds of their age.[6] Their departure seriously hampered the commercial life of Castile in particular.

The Muslims were in a stronger position. To begin with, their populations were much bigger, for not only had the Kingdom of Granada been nearly totally Islamic, but there had also been large numbers of Mudéjars living peaceably in reconquered Christian kingdoms, especially in fifteenth-century Andalusia, Valencia, and southern Aragon. Indeed, in Aragon, some towns were totally Muslim. As in the case of the Jews, a great deal of cultural assimilation and conversion (in both directions) had taken place over the centuries. Indeed, one of the reasons that the Christians attempted to make Muslims and Jews wear special garments and live in special precincts was that there was no way to distinguish them physically. Beyond that, many of the Muslims no longer spoke Arabic; there is considerable evidence by this time of Spanish texts written in Arabic script, much as Hispanic Jews after the exile would retain their Spanish language, which they called *ladino*, but write it with Hebrew letters.

The Mudéjars were also vital to Aragonese and Castilian agriculture and many were highly skilled craftsmen. The great ceramics workshops at Paterna and Manises, near Valencia, were almost entirely Muslim. Fine ware from Manises, with its metallic glazes derived from earlier Hispanic Islamic sources, was particularly prized and it became one of Valencia's principal export products to Christian markets and patrons.[7]

In Aragon, the Muslims were the great master builders. Using inexpensive materials of red brick from local clay and glazed ceramic tile, they created a distinctive style of church, and, with their Christian (and occasionally Jewish) associates, they built those churches over the entire region.[8] The plan of the churches was similar to contemporaneous stone churches in Catalonia and Valencia: of single nave with a choir over the entry bay, a polygonal apse, and side chapels in the nave located between heavy buttresses. The interiors were decorated in a style which came to be called Mudéjar, though it is technically a hybrid. The style is characterized by geometric screens or *celosias* within roundels or pointed Gothic windows, intricately carved choir rails and pulpits made of *yeseria* (plaster), and sometimes complexly inlaid wooden ceilings beneath the choir loft.[9] The brick exteriors (fig. 2)—particularly the apses and especially the bell towers—were made interesting by the incorporation of complex designs formed by the brick, using a combination of Islamic patterns, such as intersecting arches and eight-pointed stars, and more generalized geometric ones. The designs were sometimes enlivened by ceramic inserts of green, purple, white, and red (the same colors used to glaze local pottery, which was also of Mudéjar manufacture).[10] Though it would not be until the early years of the seventeenth century that the Mudéjars and the *moriscos* (Muslims who were nominal converts to Christianity) would suffer the same fate as the Jews and be expelled from the Iberian Peninsula, they too would suffer increasing marginalization as time wore on.

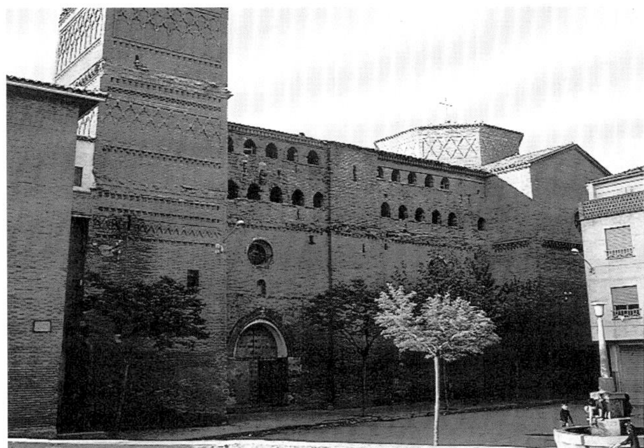

Figure 2

As for the fifteenth-century Hispanic Christian world, many upheavals would occur before the advent of the Catholic Kings and the Conquest of Granada. Dramatic changes took place in the commercial and political world of the Crown of Aragon during this period, for instance. Perhaps the most significant was a change in dynasty. The Crown of Aragon had been ruled by one line since 1118, when the count of Barcelona, Ramon Berenguer IV, married Petronila, heir to the throne of Aragon, and assumed the title to both. That line died out on the death of Martin I, in 1410, and eventually passed to his nephew, Fernando de Antequera, the son of his sister, Leonor, and the Trastámara king of Castile, Juan I.

Catalonia, by this time, was sinking into decline, as the commercial center of the Crown of Aragon shifted to Valencia. Catalan fortunes would fall still further in 1461, when Catalonia seceded from the Crown and engaged in a civil war against Fernando's second son, Juan II. It was a war that Catalonia lost a decade later, and it would not fully recover for four centuries.

Valencia, on the other hand, prospered mightily, becoming the most important commercial city on the peninsula until displaced after the discovery of the Americas and the shift of New World trade to Seville. Not only was it the chief port for Hispanic trade all around the Mediterranean (including a trade in small religious paintings and other objects, as we shall see), it also hosted thriving colonies of foreign merchants. The international character of the city was strengthened by the conquest of Naples by Alfonso V, who eventually moved there, leaving his queen, María de Castilla, behind to administer domestic affairs of the Crown of Aragon from Valencia, which became the chief conduit for their communication. Even stronger ties between Valencia and Italy were forged by the two popes of the Borja family, who came from Xátiva, south of Valencia: Calixtus III (1455–1458) and the notorious Alexander VI (1492–1503).

Iberian popes marked only the top of the Church's power pyramid in Castile and Aragon. The great bishops, abbots, and heads of military orders (now no longer so militant) were drawn from the aristocracy; often they were second sons or illegitimate offspring. The Church itself was very wealthy, owning large tracts of property that brought in substantial revenues. The Church's wealth would have a strong positive effect on the growth of the arts, for many ecclesiastics, great and small, would endow altarpieces and other church ornaments.

Castile had its own political turmoil during the first third of the century, the consequence of a weak king, Juan II, and a powerful and agressive advisor, Alvaro de Luna. Conditions did not improve after Luna's fall from power and Juan's subsequent death, in 1454, for another weak king, Enrique IV, succeeded Juan II. It was not until Enrique's death twenty years later, and the accession of his sister, Isabel, that Castile would enjoy any measure of tranquility. The marriage of Isabel to her first cousin, Fernando of Aragon, in 1469 would eventually lead to the union of the two realms, Castile and Aragon, and open a new chapter of Spanish history.

By 1500, only Navarre and Portugal remained as independent kingdoms on the Iberian Peninsula and Navarre would be annexed by Fernando in 1512. Also by 1500, the kingdoms united by the Catholic Kings had become known as Spain; alliances had already been made with the Hapsburg Empire that would ultimately lead to a foreign-born king on the Spanish throne; and Spain itself was well on the road to becoming a world power, not only in Europe, but also in the New World.

‡ ‡ ‡ ‡

As in the rest of Europe, Hispanic visual arts of the fifteenth century only reflect political, economic, and general cultural developments in part. Surviving works of painting and sculpture largely reflect religious use and content, and these are almost entirely Christian. (Both Muslims and Jews forbade the representation of the human form inside their places of worship and, in the case of the former, this prohibition seems to have extended to secular buildings as well; there are no surviving Jewish secular structures from which to judge Jewish practice).

The Christian works that have come down to us from the fifteenth century vary in quantity. In Andalusia, for example, the bulk of fifteenth-century altarpieces were replaced within two centuries by more modern ones, in part because the region enjoyed a great prosperity from New World trade, and in part because the Counter Reformation made new demands on religious expression. In Aragon and Valencia, few churches have kept their original interiors intact; they were changed during eighteenth-century interior reforms. The works which have come down to us, however, reveal regional diversities as rich as those regions' varying political histories, and a wide range of patrons who paid for them.

The spectrum is wider for the decorative arts, which run the gamut from pottery and manuscripts to decorative ironwork to furniture and textiles, both woven and painted. In the case of the Nasrids, except for architectural decoration, the surviving visual remains are entirely in this category, and include magnificent tall vases and plates of fine metallic lustreware; carved and inlaid boxes and game boards of ivory; textiles; weapons; and manuscripts.[11] Following Islamic injunctions against representing the human form, the intricate designs are almost entirely abstract.

Whether large or small, objects were seldom made simply for their inherent beauty. Indeed, the word "art" was not applied to these objects at all, for the visual arts were not among the so-called "seven liberal arts" as the fifteenth century knew them. Except for game boards and the like, almost all the objects which are now considered art and are housed in museums were utilitarian objects: made for a purpose, whether religious or secular. Even decorative tapestries and wall hangings were fashioned to keep stone dwellings warmer during cold weather, and painted screens were made to keep the sun out when it was hot.

Because of the utilitarian nature of objects, even beautiful ones, the modern idea of the art collector was virtually unknown in fifteenth-century Spain. Queen Isabel, who amassed a sizeable collection of paintings, tapestries, books, and other objects during her reign, did so from pious devotion rather than connoisseurship. A painter like Valencian Joan Reixac, who collected a Netherlandish panel of *Saint Francis,* if he thought of it beyond its contemplative function, probably valued it professionally as an exceptionally fine study object.[12] Even Canon Lluís Desplà, who was one of the first men in the Crown of Aragon to collect antiquities, collected classical inscriptions rather than sculpture.[13] For fifteenth-century collectors, the motivations for owning and valuing beautiful objects thus seem to have been conspicuous consumption and piety.

To best understand the mentality of the fifteenth-century Hispanic Christian patron, whether from Castile or

Aragon, it is instructive to look at the art in context, for though there were regional stylistic differences, the basic function of the objects was the same throughout the Iberian Peninsula.

The best place to start is in the church. The basic plan of parish churches was fairly similar throughout Spain: generally they were single-naved, although three-aisled churches were known as well. A choir was generally located above the entry bay, while the apse (or apses, if there were three aisles) were polygonal. Most churches by this period had chapels, which were located between heavy buttresses. In the Crown of Aragon, the proportions of these structures were fairly squat, and the walls heavy. In Castile, they were somewhat more vertically oriented, though not to the extent seen in European Gothic churches.

Cathedrals were different. The majority were built over a long period of time, often over several centuries. Some of those built in Castile followed Northern European Gothic models (the Cathedrals of Toledo and Burgos, for example), while those in the Crown of Aragon tended to be wider, more solid and boxy, while retaining Gothic-style pointed vaults. At least two of these cathedrals were peculiarly Hispanic: the Cathedrals of Seville and Zaragoza both have rectangular plans that evolved from the rectangular sites of the mosques that they replaced. In Castile, cathedrals characteristically had richly decorated portals; stained glass windows (in the great cathedrals); lacy, Gothic tracery spires; and, toward the end of the century, *retablo*-like sculpted themes on the principal facades. In the Crown of Aragon, cathedral exteriors were somewhat more austere and heavy, though doorways might have some sculptural decoration, and many churches had rich stained-glass windows (though not the "glass curtains" of the Cathedral of León). A final feature of cathedrals and monastic churches, beginning in the late fourteenth and early fifteenth centuries, was the location of choirs in the last nave bays before the transept. This placement tended to block the view of the high altar for anyone entering the church through the main portal, but the screen separating the choir from the nave was often richly carved, and the backs and undersides of the singers' wooden stalls were also adorned with carved images.

But the architectural decoration of the church was only the beginning. Inside the church was a profusion of decorated objects, large and small, of varying materials. The most spectacular were certainly the *retablos*. These large and complex altarpieces had evolved over the course of the late fourteenth and fifteenth centuries to towering dimensions, in Castile following the shape of the apse (fig. 3), in the Crown of Aragon forming a flat, stepped screen in front of it (fig. 4). Surrounding a set scheme of painted or sculpted segments, which varied in format by region, there was a unifying, sculpted frame of sumptuous Gothic tracery enclosed within an outer frame of *guardapolvos*, or tilted dust guards, which held all components in place and, in

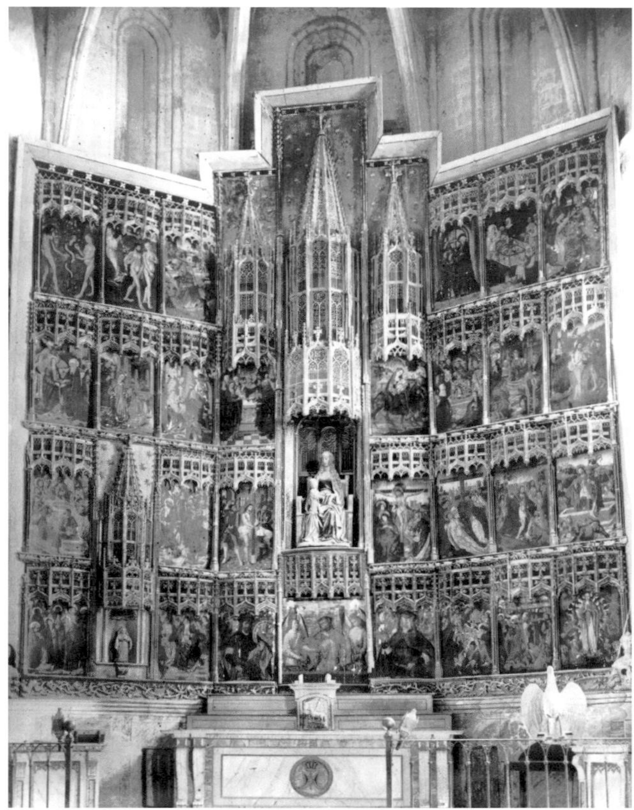

Figure 3

effect, formed a bridge between architecture and sculpture or painting.[14]

A few wealthy churches boasted *retablos* of precious metal, for instance, the still-extant high altar *retablo* in the Cathedral of Girona. Some were made of alabaster, particularly in the Crown of Aragon: the high altar of the Cathedral of Zaragoza comes to mind. More were made of wood, polychromed and gilded, as were the frames, as at Toledo Cathedral (fig. 5). Most numerous were *retablos* that were wholly painted or mostly painted with one or more sculpted images in its center, which could function as a sacred icon. In the Crown of Aragon, a sculpted or painted tabernacle for reserve hosts was also placed in the center of the *banco*, the lowest strip of paintings. The painting was generally in brilliant colors, with gold grounds behind the figures, and often with gilt accessories and garments on the painted or polychromed sculpted figures as well.

Iberian churches would have been spectacular had they had just one *retablo* over the high altar, but many of the side chapels also had painted, or occasionally sculpted, *retablos*. The subject of these altarpieces would have been the saint to whom the chapel was dedicated, usually the patron of the donor or donors. (Similarly, the altarpieces of the high altar would be dedicated to the patron saint of the church itself.) Chapel *retablos* would have had a combination of narrative and iconic images of the principal subject, either standing or enthroned, and generally combined with an image of *Christ on the Cross*. Replacing the tabernacle of the *retablos*

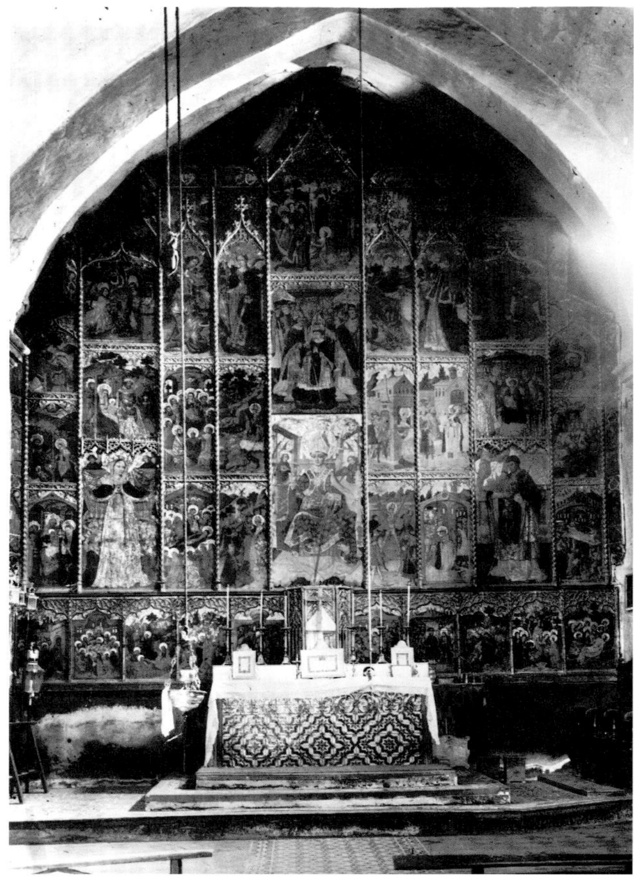

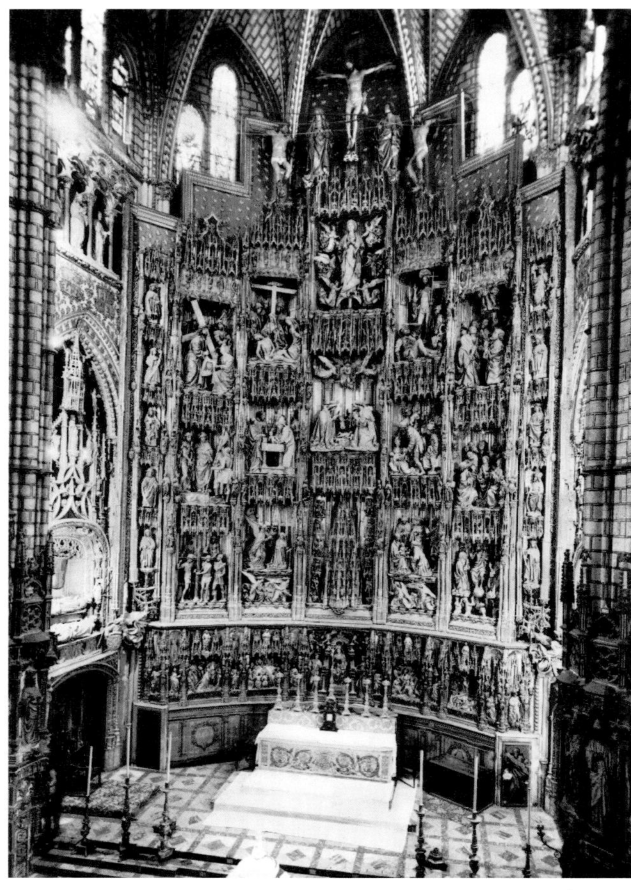

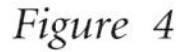

Figure 4

Figure 5

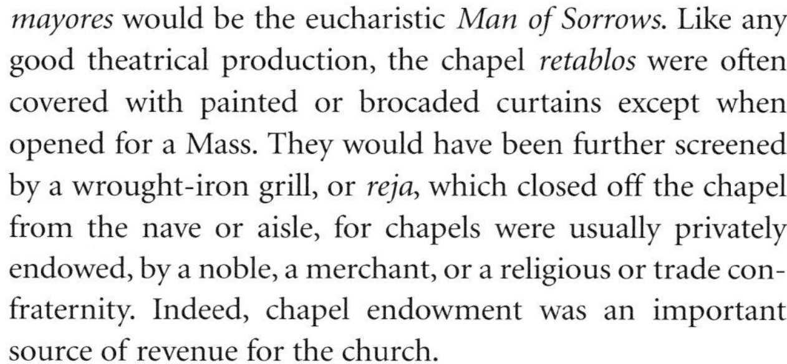

mayores would be the eucharistic *Man of Sorrows*. Like any good theatrical production, the chapel *retablos* were often covered with painted or brocaded curtains except when opened for a Mass. They would have been further screened by a wrought-iron grill, or *reja*, which closed off the chapel from the nave or aisle, for chapels were usually privately endowed, by a noble, a merchant, or a religious or trade confraternity. Indeed, chapel endowment was an important source of revenue for the church.

Donors' coats of arms might be painted on wooden shields and hung on the chapel walls, or might be painted directly on the walls themselves. In some areas (most notably parts of Castile, Asturias, León, Galicia, and Navarre), chapel walls were all painted with religious scenes, though never to the extent that they were in Italy, and never so much as to overwhelm the *retablo*.

On occasion, the *retablo* was replaced by a single devotional panel or image, normally one of the Virgin, but occasionally of a single saint. Some of these were icons with a fervent devotional following. These are found particularly in Andalusia, examples being the *Virgen de los Remedios* and the *Virgen de la Antigua*, both in the Cathedral of Seville. (It is hard to consider these images to be works of art in the modern sense because they have been so renewed and repainted over the years that their original appearance is difficult to determine. In this they anticipate later Andalusian carved images of saints, like the *Virgen de la Macarena*, who boasts a considerable wardrobe that has been updated continually, even to this day.) Other solitary images were less exalted, but provided a more singular focus for worship than a multi-paneled *retablo*. These images would have been painted or carved—following the same techniques and often in the same workshops as the *retablos* themselves.

In addition to the decorations placed behind the altars and on the walls, the altars themselves and the areas around them were filled with objects, some permanent, others displayed only on special occasions. The painted altar frontal was still occasionally found in fifteenth-century churches, though by this period it appears to have been dying out, probably because the pictorial richness of the *retablo* overwhelmed it. Still, the fronts and sides of the altars were often draped with brocaded or occasionally painted cloths. The Mass provided an occasion for high theater, a drama that was reinforced by dazzling accessories and ceremonial objects. Necessary vessels for Communion were the chalice and paten, for wine and wafer; these were made of the finest materials the parish or cathedral chapter could afford. For special occasions, a monstrance was produced to display the host; as elaborate as any Gothic spire, it would be made of precious metal. A metal, stone, or wooden crucifix was also necessary for the Mass (though a painted one within the altarpiece apparently sometimes served as substitute), and

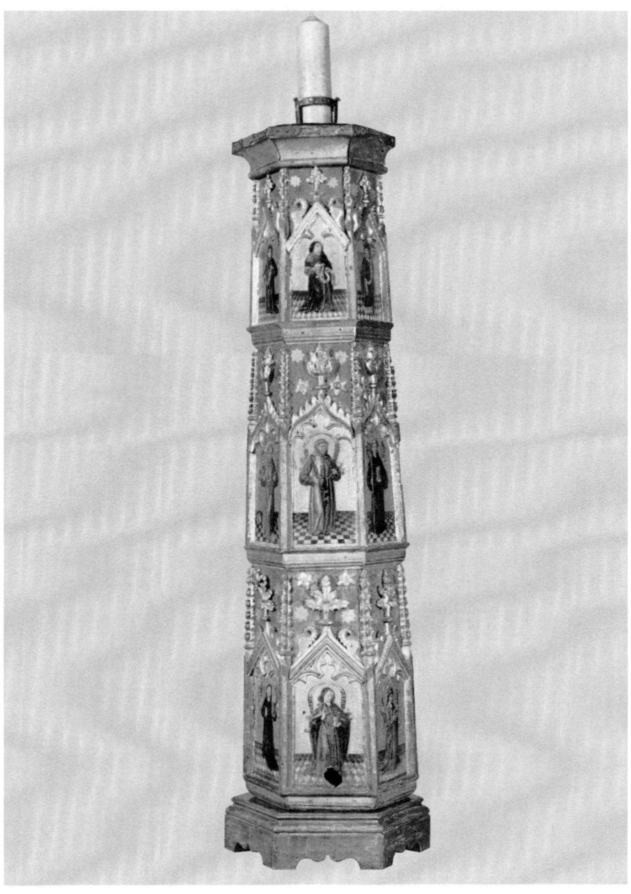

Figure 6

the church might also have a finely wrought processional cross. Add to this the huge, often profusely illuminated choir books and the rich, brocaded vestments of the clergy, and a wonderful sense of spectacle would have surrounded and enveloped the worshiper, enhancing the fervor of the Mass itself.

Relics and other donations further embellished the interiors. Relics of the patron saint of a church—or those of another saint if one of the patron was not available—were traditionally built into the altar; additional relics donated by proud individuals would be displayed in decorated containers called reliquaries. These ranged from simple painted wooden coffers to rich gold-and-bejeweled confections of the most exquisite goldsmith's craft. Ex-votos were also given to churches, usually in thanks for prayers having been answered at a time of difficulty; they were often objects precious to the donor, but they were not necessarily art objects. Such donations varied greatly: from the shell, silver, and enamel ship model (originally a spice container) donated to the Cathedral Zaragoza by the Valencian pirate Juan de Torellas[15] to the crocodile skin which Münzer saw in the Monastery of Guadalupe, donated by a Portuguese gentleman who had been saved from its jaws by invoking the Virgin Mary.[16]

Church interiors were lavishly lit with artificial illumination. Great candles—expensive donations of the finest white wax—were sometimes ensconced in large candlesticks for special occasions (fig. 6) and more modest donations of smaller candles were ordinarily arranged in banks. Oil lamps also provided light. The late fifteenth-century German traveler Hieronymus Münzer spoke of sixteen lamps of silver and silver gilt which burned day and night before the *retablo mayor* of the Monastery of Guadalupe, and more than one hundred and twenty lamps burned in the Chapel of the Virgin in the Monastery of St. Augustine in Valencia.[17]

Lastly, churches were decorated by tombs. Though ordinary citizens were buried in cemeteries, notables—usually ecclesiastic and secular aristocrats—would be granted the honor of burial within the churches themselves. Burials could be in wall tombs along the nave or aisles (if there were no side chapels), along the ambulatory in cathedrals, or within a chapel endowed by the deceased's family. The remains were placed in stone sarcophagi, which frequently bore the coats of arms of the deceased or a series of religious scenes from the life of a favorite patron saint. The sarcophagus usually bore a recumbent image of the deceased, in full vestments, armor, or robes (or best gown, if an aristocratic woman), with a pillow beneath the head, and sometimes a dog (a symbol of fidelity), or a lion at the feet. The sarcophagus and effigy were placed in wall niches, which were sometimes elaborately decorated with tracery. The most influential and powerful people were interred in free-standing tombs, which necessitated larger chapels. Here the sarcophagi were richer, and the effigy of the deceased might be surrounded by allegorical figures, saints, or pages. A particularly elaborate example are the tombs of Alvaro de Luna and his wife, Juana Pimentel, which were commissioned by their daughter María in 1488, and placed, along with more modest wall tombs of less exalted family members, in the enormous family chapel in the ambulatory of Toledo Cathedral (fig. 7). To the splendor of the tombs were added temporary funerary embellishments. At the time of interment, the chapels that received the burials would have been festooned with coats of arms, decorated cloths, canopies, and candles, further enhancing the ornamentation inside the church, if only for a short time.[18]

Art with religious content was by no means confined to the church and monastery. Wealthy people frequently had a private chapel, and the less wealthy might have a small altar in the home. Certain types of religious paintings were fashioned, then, for private use. Triptychs, when found in Spain, were generally small in scale, and intended for private devotion. Small individual paintings, particularly images of the Virgin and the so-called *Veronica* (the face of Christ on a white veil) probably served the same function. Manuscripts for personal prayer were also made, and they transcended Christianity: copies of the Koran, Jewish books of daily prayer, and the Haggadot, the text used at the Passover seder, are all documented in fifteenth-century Spain. Because privately-owned Jewish manuscripts were not taken into the synagogue, there was no prohibition on making human images, and many of these works were profusely illustrated. The illuminations for these were sometimes produced by Jewish workshops, but other times only the Hebrew texts were executed by Jewish scribes; the pictures came out of the studios of Christian manuscript illuminators. The iconographical consequences of this dual production are extremely revealing, for although illuminations in Jewish bibles and Haggadot and Christian Old Testament manuscripts were sometimes based on the same text, different episodes were selected for illustration. Christians generally illustrated scenes that they believed prefigured New Testament events, such as the *Temptation of Adam and Eve* and the *Expulsion from Paradise*, while the range of Jewish illustration is far wider.[19]

In the fifteenth century, the line between secular and religious life and its imagery was often blurred, for religion permeated everyday life to a degree beyond contemporary

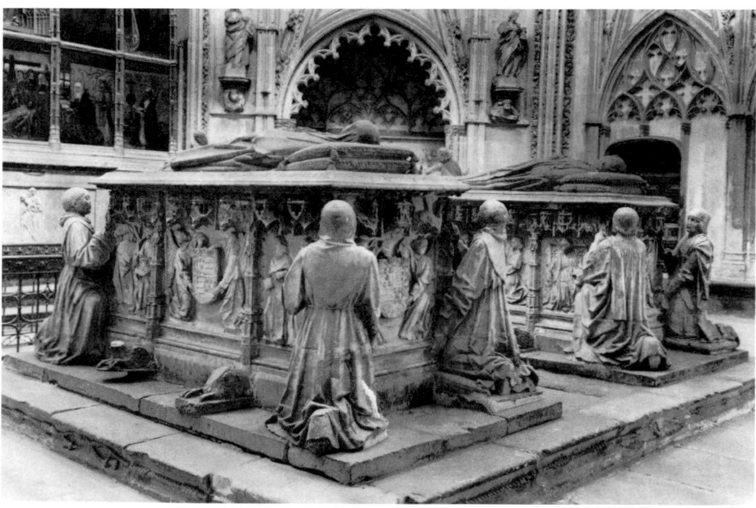

Figure 7

imagining, unless one is a fundamentalist Christian, or ultra-Orthodox Jew or Muslim, living within a closed community. Prosperous Christian homes were decorated with painted and carved furniture, window screens, and tapestries not too different in function from contemporary interior decoration, but quite different in their subject matter. A fascinating inventory from the two houses owned by the Barcelona merchant Antonio Cases, made at his death in 1448, reveals something of this variety. It includes a number of Flemish imports, including an image of the Virgin, a carved bench embellished with foliage, a brocaded bedspread, a six-branched candelabrum with the image of the Virgin and Child, as well as a Venetian mirror (broken!). Even more interesting is the assortment of painted furniture, cloth screens, hangings, and canopies, whose subject matter includes scenes from the life and passion of Christ; images of several saints including St. George and St. Michael; Alexander the Great; a marinescape of towers, ships and galleys; wild men fighting on horseback; assorted birds and animals; the Virgin Mary; and "men and women who bathe in a bath."[20] Bed hangings and screens were adorned with secular and religious scenes of no apparent coherence, and the juxtaposition of such diverse subject matters speaks for itself, though it is still not clear how typical this collection of goods was of its time and place.

A great deal of non-figural housewares was also produced in this era. Mudéjar ceramic vessels from the Valencian towns of Manises and Paterna were the crockery of their day, and the wealthier citizens of Castile, if not Aragon, probably had access to Nasrid silk hangings and pile carpets as well. Though a number of the pile carpets were imported from Turkey (one appears in the center panel of Bernat Martorell's *retablo mayor* painted between 1437 and 1442 for the chapel of the Castle of Púbol and now in the Museu d'Art, Girona), far more were of indigenous Andalusian Mudéjar and Nasrid manufacture. Some of these were based on Anatolian designs, but others, woven on commission for the aristocracy and royalty, had Hispanic coats of arms incorporated into their patterns.[21]

An examination of documents on fifteenth-century painters in the Crown of Aragon reveals a large variety of other painted objects manufactured for daily use. An entire industry developed for making storage boxes with painted lids (similar to Italian cassoni of the same period) as well as painted clogs, bridles, saddles, and shields. It is therefore not surprising that the brotherhood of painters in Barcelona was affiliated with the bridlemakers' guild, and that the painters of Valencia were concentrated around the *plaça dels caixers*, or the Plaza of the Box Makers.

It is hard to estimate the size of production for fifteenth-century painted objects because such a small portion of it has survived. Probably more large altarpieces have survived than anything else, and for these, the late scholar José Gudiol Ricart estimated that the two thousand *retablo* works that have survived to the twentieth century represent only a hundredth of the original production.[22] Painted furniture is rare, painted cloth rarer. It is difficult to imagine the vast quantity of painted panels, cloth, furniture, clogs, coats of arms, storage boxes, and other painted items that the industrious workshops of fifteenth-century Spain produced.

Such a vast industry required many workers. Most studies of fifteenth-century Hispanic painting have been concerned only with *retablos* and their makers. Those painters were at the top of the artisans' pyramid, and these masters and their workshops could command the highest prices. By the last quarter of the century, *retablo* painters in the large cities of both Castile and the Crown of Aragon had to undergo a set period of apprenticeship and pass stiff examinations in order to practice their trade. Those who succeeded performed mainly contract work, for the altarpieces were generally executed on commission from individuals or groups.[23] Those who failed often ended up as contract workers in other masters' shops, their work a lesser collaboration appearing only under the shop master's name.

Lower down in the hierarchy were cloth painters, about whom considerably less is known. The few extant fifteenth-century guild regulations state that cloth masters had to pass competency tests as well.[24] But little painted cloth from this period survives, and most that does was ecclesiastic work from the shops of those *retablo* painters who were also licensed to paint on fabric (for instance, Pedro Berruguete's organ shutters, now in the Prado). Antonio Cases' inventory makes clear, however, that many of the works from the cloth painters' studios were secular, and as there appear to be few, if any surviving contracts dealing with this production, we can only assume that it was painting done on speculation, perhaps like interior decoration painting today. The generic descriptions in the Cases' inventory suggest that the same designs were reproduced over and over again, giving the idea that these secular painted cloths were made to be used until they wore out—unlike the altarpieces, which were fashioned with posterity in mind. As for the painters of bridles, boxes, coats of arms, and clogs, even less is known, except that many of them appear to have specialized in particular products: the inventories of the painter Ramon Torrent, who died in Zaragoza in 1325, indicates that he was an artisan who painted mainly crucifixes, single images of saints, and coats of arms.[25] There is little to suggest that the situation was much different a century later.

Much scholarship has been done on the great patrons—the monarchs, nobles, and upper-echelon clergy who endowed churches and chapels, footed the bill for sumptuous *retablos*, and ordered sumptuous tombs. Some idea of the splendor in which these luminaries lived can be garnered from Münzer's description of the house of Cardinal Pedro de Mendoza at Guadalajara:

> *The house of the cardinal, on the outskirts of Guadalajara, is one of the most beautiful of all of Spain. I have seen many grand palaces of cardinals in Rome, but in all my life I have never seen one as beautiful and with such well distributed rooms. It has two beautiful superimposed cloisters, with little rooms and chambers, all with gilded* artesonados *(wooden inlaid ceilings) and with diverse colors mixed with blue, each* artesonado *being different from the other, two summer rooms which open to the garden with marble columns and resplendent with so much gold that it is difficult to believe. Oh, what a majestic chapel!, long, although not very wide, on whose altar are exquisite paintings of Saint Peter and Saint Paul and the blessed Virgin, and at the sides Saint Gregory and Saint Helen with the cross, which carried a title like a cardinal; a beautiful garden in the center of which is a fountain with which everything can be watered, an immense aviary, partly covered, part surrounded by copper wires, in which there are so many kinds of birds, that it is impossible to describe them . . . I think that in the world there is no more splendid house. He left incomparable riches, because he was rich by inheritance, by the archbishopric of Toledo, by the bishopric of Sigüenza, and by the cardinalship. He had many other benefices. He was an intimate of the king, and of an austere life; but in his other spending he was very splendid.*[26]

The patronage of these courtly personages is well known. Much has been made, for example, of Cardinal Rodrigo de Borja, the future Pope Alexander VI, who, when he made a triumphal visit to Valencia in 1472, brought with him the Italian painters Paolo da San Leocadio, Francesco Pagano, and Riccardo Quartararo to paint in the Cathedral.[27] Most studied of all royal patrons were, of course, the Catholic Kings, particularly Queen Isabel, whose taste for Northern European painters, sculptors, and architects was also reflected in the tastes of her noble Castilian contemporaries.[28]

More problematic is gauging the amount of influence these great patrons had on the general panorama of the arts on the Iberian Peninsula during the fifteenth century. The conventional notion of style in art history is one of trickle-down—from the great patrons to the less informed tastes of the general populace. Influenced by this idea, art historians earlier in this century characterized most Spanish painting and sculpture during the second half of the fifteenth century as "Hispano-Flemish" (just as they had called late-fourteenth-century painting "Italo-Gothic"), as if the entire Iberian Peninsula were an artistic wasteland, ready to absorb like a thirsty sponge more sophisticated styles imported by the courtly elite. The reality is far more complicated.

To begin with, several levels of patronage existed simultaneously on the Iberian Peninsula, and the secular and ecclesiastic aristocracy was only one of them. The merchant class certainly played a part, too, for not only did merchants act as patrons, endowing a chapel in their parish if wealthy enough, but in cities like Valencia and Burgos, they also imported the sorts of furniture, ornaments, and small painted devotional panels mentioned in Antonio Cases' inventory. But, particularly in the Crown of Aragon, there was an even broader base of more modest individuals who contributed to the cost of altarpieces and other sacred objects. Both trade guilds and brotherhoods, as well as religious lay brotherhoods, endowed chapels and the ceremonial objects within them, each member contributing a share. The same was true in small parishes, where it was common for each parishioner to be assessed a modest sum toward the painting or sculpting of the high altar *retablo*.

There remains the question of local style and traditions. In the Crown of Aragon, regional styles of painting had evolved right along with the evolution of the *retablo*. Though there were fourteenth-century roots in a general style which came in part from Italy, particularly in Catalonia, Valencia, and the Balearic Islands, they had evolved within one generation to the peculiar needs of the large, multi-sectioned altarpiece as it was developing all over the Iberian Peninsula. This development was, in turn, dependent on the evolving plan of the Iberian parish church, whose open, boxy space and modest ornamentation encouraged richly painted and sculpted decorations in its religious imagery.

By the fifteenth century, individual panels and images within the *retablos* had become fewer and bigger, and frame ornamentation had become more elaborate, following the general development of late Gothic ornamentation. But, in Aragon and Catalonia, the basic style of painting and sculpture—with its lack of illusory perspective in narratives and reliefs—and its exaltation of flat patterning, was a natural evolution from the earlier styles. Part of the reason for this was Aragon's inland location and Catalonia's later fifteenth-centruy commercial and political decline, which caused it to turn inward. Though painters and sculptors of the region freely consulted German and Flemish woodcuts and engravings for compositions, a common practice in this period, they only superficially took anything from their style. This argument leaves aside isolated cases like Lluís Dalmau's *Virgin of the Councilors*, which was specifically contracted for in a Netherlandish style.

In Valencia the case was different because of its increasing importance as an international trade and political center. Luxury goods were imported to Valencia from many diverse places, and foreign merchant colonies brought their own tastes with them. The Mediterranean policies of Alfonso V and the elevation of the two Borja popes, both using Valencia as a conduit to the rest of the peninsula, attracted international attention to the city. It is for these reasons that Valencian painting, sculpture, and minor arts were so cosmopolitan, open not only to Northem European luxury goods and small painted panels, but also to the growing movement of the early Renaissance in Italy. Knowledgeable painters like Rodrigo and Francesc de Osona were quick to appropriate the use of oil glazes, which enabled them to paint the sort of rich fabrics and jewels common in the work of their Flemish contemporaries. They also attempted the illusion of consistent space, which would have been both demanded and appreciated by sophisticated Valencian audiences.

Less is known about developments of style in the Kingdom of Castile for few altarpieces before 1400 survive from the Castilian territories, though architectural sculpture indicates a tradition of ties with France (not surprising given Castile's political ties with Northern Europe). It may be that Castile lacked a strong tradition of painting and sculpting altarpieces in the fourteenth-century, though the sophisticated formats of fifteenth-century tombs and *retablos* suggests a considerable period of evolution. But if the term "Hispano-Flemish" can be applied to fifteenth-century painting and sculpture anywhere on the Iberian Peninsula, it is here. Certainly it is true that a large number of Northern European sculptors and painters were enticed to the region by fat commissions from the nobility. The list of names of the foreign masters is long, but a sampling includes sculptors and master builders Juan Alemán, Felipe and Daniel de Bruselas, Hanequin de Bruselas and his brother Egas Cueman, and "Petit Juan" (all of whom worked in Toledo), Gil de Siloe, Simon and Juan de Colonia, and the painters Jorge Inglés, Juan de Flandes, and Michel Sittow. It appears that in the majority of cases, these masters worked mainly for royalty or the high nobility. Some, like Gil de Siloe, settled permanently in Castile, while others, like Sittow, a court artist to his bones, left the Iberian Peninsula to continue their careers at other aristocratic centers.

In Castile, the interest in Northern European art appears to have reached beyond the aristocracy. Flemish conventions of drapery and landscape, as well as appropriated compositions from prints and sometimes from paintings, are found on a wide range of altarpieces, not only in Castile itself, but also in León and Andalusia. It must be remembered, however, that in western Europe in the fifteenth century, Netherlandish art was almost universally adored and, when possible, emulated. In this respect, Castile was simply part of an international "Euroculture."

But it was Euroculture with its own twist. Castilian paintings and reliefs tend to flatten space much as do their Aragonese counterparts, and probably for the same reason: the multi-paneled form of the *retablo*. There is also another factor, both in Castile and Andalusia and in Aragon and Catalonia, which is peculiar to Iberian culture: the profusion of *retablo* surface ornamentation. Many painted panels, for example, appear to have some sort of patterning over the entire surface. A good example is Jaume Huguet's *Coronation of St. Augustine*, painted for the church of Sant Agosti Vell in Barcelona, and now in the Museu d'Art de Catalunya (fig. 8). In this painting, every vestment has a different pattern, the floor tiles and the cloth behind Augustine are also patterned, and the cope orphreys, mitres, and gold ground are modeled in *embutido* (modeled and gilded gesso). This sort of patterning has much in common with the profusion of patterns on Mudéjar pottery, and with the incredibly complex juxtaposition of carved stucco, patterned tile, and carved and inlaid wood found in the Nasrid palaces of the Alhambra.

The presence of three religions and cultures on the Iberian Peninsula for so many centuries led to a cultural blending which was peculiar to Spain. We see it today mostly in Christian monuments and art objects, probably because so much of what has survived from fifteenth-century Spain is Christian, but it must have been very widespread among all three groups. At times the interchange is noticeable in a very direct way. The fourteenth-century Synagogue of Samuel Halevi Abulafia in Toledo (now called El Tránsito),

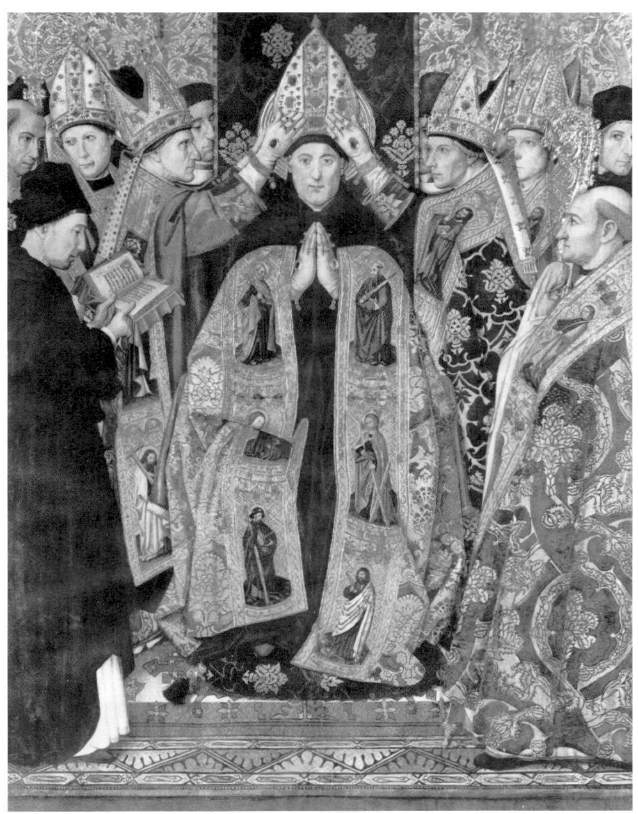

Figure 8

for instance, is decorated with stucco carving in the spirit, if not the design, of contemporaneous Nasrid buildings; there are also affinities with Christian buildings dating from the period of Pedro III ("el Cruel") of Castile, of whom Abulafia was both financial advisor and victim.[29] The synagogue has an *artesonado* ceiling similar to those in contemporaneous Christian churches—the spectacular nave vault of Teruel Cathedral comes to mind, but there are much closer examples in Castile.

In other instances, the allusions are more subtle. The panels of the *banco* of the *retablo mayor* from Santa María de Arbás in Mayorga have gilded backgrounds with geometric interlacings characteristic of the window screens of both the Alhambra and the Aragonese Mudéjar church of Santa María Maluenda. Less overt though far more complex are some late fifteenth-century examples of architecture and sculpture usually called "Isabeline," in honor of the Castilian queen. For instance, the entire *retablo* facade of the Colegio de San Gregorio at Valladolid is webbed with a complex variety of Gothic tracery, foliage, and embedded figures. In Gil de Siloe's *retablo mayor* in the Carthusian monastery of Miraflores, the traditional compartmentalization of the *retablo* dissolves in an even more extreme way. The viewer's first impression of this altarpiece, before any attempt can be made to decipher it, is of a sheer wall of decorative pattern surrounding a massive crucifix.

Though a similar use of busy pattern would in part govern the early sixteenth-century architectural style known as "plateresque," forces were already at work by 1500 that would change the appearance and content of Hispanic art forever. Fernando and Isabel's policies of conversion and expulsion would soon rid the Iberian Peninsula of the Jews and Muslims who had been a cultural and political presence for centuries, and with them departed the religious sensibilities that shaped their visual arts. Trastámara marriages with the Hapsburgs would bring strong cultural and intellectual currents into Spain of a very different sort, including a strong dose of the Italian humanism that would come to influence sixteenth-century European artistic culture as Netherlandish art had done in the fifteenth century. Lastly, the Counter Reformation would change the vocabulary and iconography of Catholic art. All of these elements would lead to what is often called Spain's "Golden Age," but in the process, the often wildly contradictary fusion of disparate religious and regional elements which characterize medieval Spanish art would be lost.

1. The terms "Castile" and "Kingdom of Castile" will be used in this essay to mean the entire territory defined in this paragraph, including the old kingdom of León.

2. Not included in this account is Sicily, conquered by Pedro III in 1282, though it was often ruled by a junior branch of the Aragonese line.

3. An excellent and concise account of Spanish history from this period can be found in Joseph F. O'Callaghan, *A History of Medieval Spain*, Ithaca, N.Y., Cornell University Press, 1975, especially Part V and Epilogue, 521–677.

4. Ytzak Baer, *A History of Jews in Christian Spain*, II, Philadelphia, The Jewish Publication Society of America, 1966, 95ff.

5. Norman Roth, "Jewish *Conversos* in Medieval Spain: Some Misconceptions and New Information," in *Marginated Groups in Spanish and Portuguese History*, Minneapolis, The Society for Spanish and Portuguese Historical Studies, 1989, 23–24.

6. Some estimates place this number as high as 800,000. See O'Callaghan, 1975, 671.

7. Manises ware is discussed in greater detail in catalogue no. 7. An interesting case is a Passover plate from Manises, now in the Jerusalem Museum; it was evidently a special order, but the ceramist was not conversant with Hebrew, and so the inscription has some errors. See illustration in Jay Levinson, ed., *Circa 1492: Art in the Age of Exploration*, New Haven, Yale University Press, cat. no. 54, 172.

8. Presumably Muslim builders also constructed mosques and synagogues of similar materials that have not survived.

9. The popular name for these wooden ceilings was *artesonado*, which means "trough-shaped" and describes the shape of the original ceilings. (A good example is the nave vault of the Cathedral of Tereul.) The term has been extended to flat ceilings as well.

10. For a general overview of Aragonese Mudéjar architecture and its decoration, see Gonzalo M. Borrás Gualis, *Arte Mudéjar Aragonés*, Zaragoza, Caja de Ahorros y Monte de Piedad de Zaragoza, Aragón y Rioja, n.d., 1985(?). Borrás cites one wonderful example of Islamic "sabotage" of a Christian church, that of Santa María, Maluenda, where its master builder, Yuçaf Abdolmelic, inserted the Arabic phrase "There is no other god than God; Mahoma is the messenger of God. There is only . . . God." right along with the Latin "Ave Maria" in a frieze around the decorative wooden ceiling underneath the choir loft! Borrás, 1985(?), II, 215–216.

11. For fine examples of these objects, see Jerrilyn D. Dodds, ed. *Al-Andalus: The Art of Islamic Spain*, New York, The Metropolitan Museum of Art, 1992, particularly the catalogue of exhibited objects, 264–391.

12. Lluís Gomis, "Pintores valentinos, su cronología y documentación," *Anales del Centro de Cultura Valenciana*, XXV (1964), 98.

13. See Agustí Duran I Sanpere, *Barcelona i la seva història*, I, Barcelona, Curial, 1942, 408.

14. For a study of painted *retablos* and their regional variations, see Judith Berg Sobré, *Behind the Altar Table*, Columbia, Mo., University of Missouri Press, 1989.

15. Illustrated in *Reyes y Mecenas. Los Reyes Católicos, Maximiliano I y los Inicios de la Casa de Austria en España*, Madrid, Ministerio de Cultura, 1992.

16. Münzer, 1951, 92.

17. Hieronymus Münzer, *Viaje por España y Portugal, 1494–95*, (translated by José López Toro), Madrid, Colección Almenara, 1951, 16, 92.

18. Fifteenth-century obsequies were subdued in comparison to later Spanish rites. See Stephen Orso, *Art and Death at the Spanish Hapsburg Court: The Royal Exequies for Philip IV*, Columbia, Mo., 1989, especially his first two chapters.

19. See Gabrielle Sed-Rajana, *The Hebrew Bible in Medieval Illuminated Manuscripts*, New York, Rizzoli, 1987, 7–8, 155–156.

20. José María Madurell Marimón, "El pintor Lluís Borrassà, su vida, su tiempo sus seguidores y sus obras, III, addenda al apéndice documental," *Anales y Boletin de los Museos de Barcelona*, X, 1952, 303–310.

21. M. S. Dimand, *Oriental Rugs in the Metropolitan Museum of Art*, New York, The Metropolitan Museum of Art, 1973, 251–261.

22. José Guidol Ricart, *Ars Hispaniae, IX: Pintura Gótica*, Madrid, Espasa Calpe, 1955, 13.

23. Most surviving contracts of the fifteenth century come from the Crown of Aragon, where notaries generally bound their documents into books. In Castile, notaries usually spindled their contracts throughout this period, and so few survive.

24. For a summary of brotherhood regulations, see Berg Sobré, 1989, 12–17.

25. Mariano Serrano y Sanz, "Documentos relativos a la pintura en Aragón durante los siglos XIV y XV," *Revista de Archivos*, Bibliotecas y Museos 36 (1917), 105–111.

26. Münzer, 1951, 116 (author's translation into English).

27. For the latest account of this visit, see Ximo Company i Climent, *El mundo de los Osona*, Valencia, Museu Sant Pius V, 1994, 94–99.

28. The quincentenary of the first voyage of Columbus produced a rash of exhibitions and publications dealing with royal and aristocratic patronage in the age of Queen Isabel. See in particular, Fernando Checa, "Poder y piedad: patronos y mecenas en la introducción del renacimiento en España," *Reyes y Mecenas*, 1992, 21–54.

29. Esther W. Goldman, "Samuel Halevi Abulafia's Synagogue (El Tránsito) in Toledo," Jewish Art, *Journal of the Center for Jewish Art*, 18 (1992), Jerusalem, The Hebrew University, 58–69.

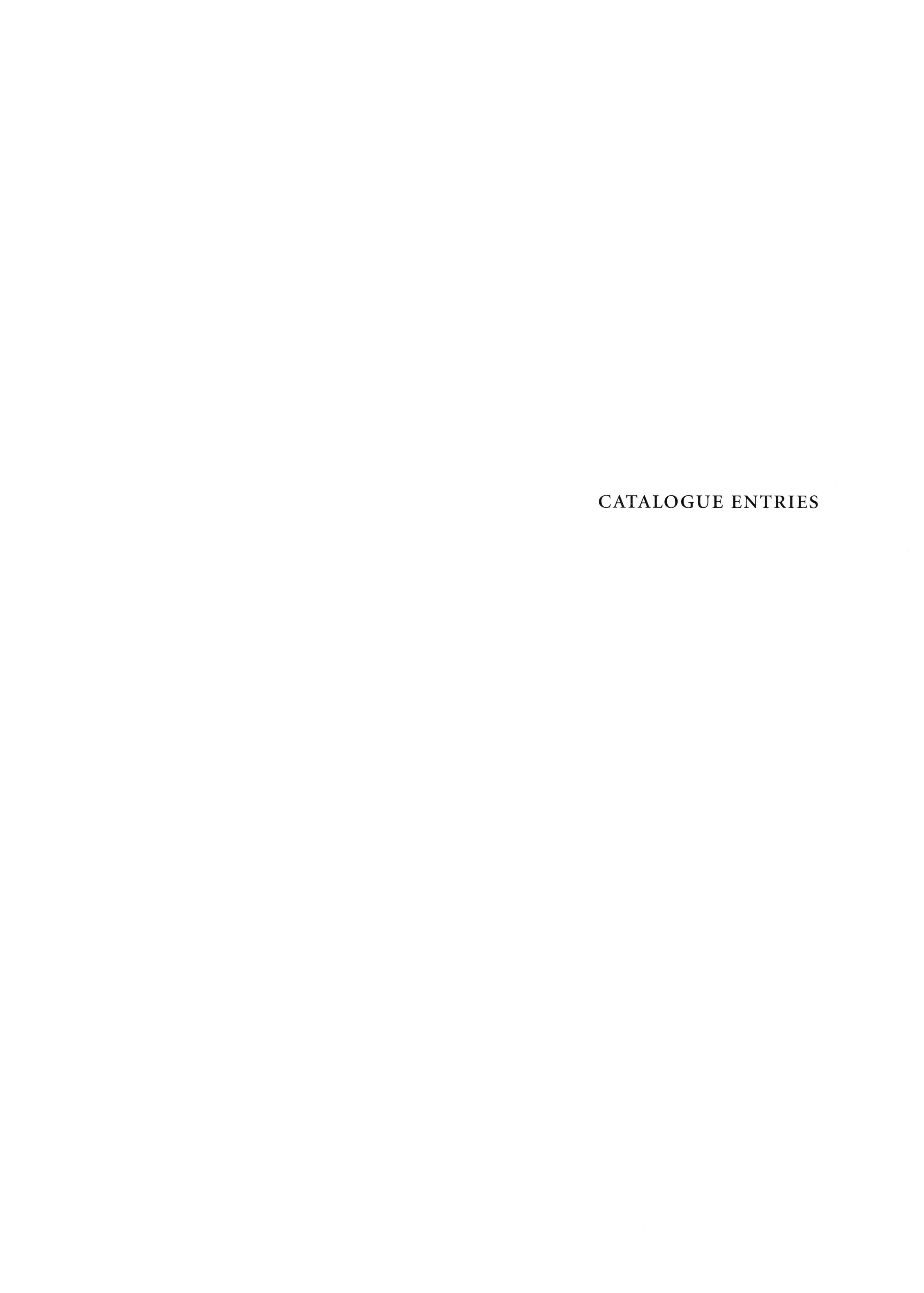

CATALOGUE ENTRIES

Catalogue Nos. 1a and 1b

BARTOLOMÉ DE CÁRDENAS, ALSO CALLED BARTOLOMÉ BERMEJO

Active in various cities in the Crown of Aragon (Valencia, Daroca, Zaragoza, Barcelona), ca. 1468–1495

Center Panel and Narrative from the Retablo of St. Engracia

1a. St. Engracia, ca. 1475
Oil on conifer panel
64 1/4 x 28 1/2 in.
Isabella Stewart Gardner Museum, Boston
P19e25

1b. The Capture of St. Engracia, ca. 1475
Oil on conifer panel
43 x 26 in.
San Diego Museum of Art
Gift of Misses Anne R. and Amy Putnam
1941:101

These two panels come from the same *retablo,* dedicated to St. Engracia. The single figure of St. Engracia (fig. 1-1) stands before a thronelike niche adorned with Mudéjar eight-pointed stars, which in turn is placed in front of a gold ground, embossed at its borders with an oak leaf pattern. She is sumptuously dressed in a wine-colored velvet underskirt, a brocaded robe bordered in ermine, a jacket also of wine velvet with ermine borders and fur cuffs, and a deep blue cape with an embroidered and jeweled border, lined with green brocade. Her golden hair is braided, and wound over an elaborate pearl-encrusted headdress topped with a crown and bound, under the chin, with a transparent veil whose ends flare out behind the headdress at the back. She wears a necklace of overlapping gold circles and a ring on the third finger of her left hand. In her right hand she holds a martyr's palm, and her left hand, which catches up her brocaded robe, also holds the instrument of her martyrdom, a large spike. She also has a halo of concentric rings of *embutido,* raised and gilded gesso. This panel was placed in the center of the *retablo.*

The second panel (fig. 1-3) is a narrative, which would have flanked the effigy of *St. Engracia.* It depicts St. Engracia's capture by Dacian, the Roman proconsul of Zaragoza. The scene takes place on a city street of dirt. Engracia, riding a small pony, is detained by two aides of Dacian. A dwarfish aide grabs the pony's bridle while a second, taller henchman lays hands on the saint as if to pull her off her horse. Behind, a crowd of male onlookers watch. Dacian himself, dressed in a tunic, a brocaded shirt, and a turban with a mock-Kufic inscription, directs the operation on horseback, gesturing with his staff. Engracia wears the same dress, headdress, and halo as she does on the effigy.

The cult of St. Engracia is confined to the Iberian Peninsula and extreme southern France, and she enjoyed particular popularity in Aragon. She first appears in Aurelius Prudentius's *Peristephanon* (where she is called Encratis) as a Christian virgin who is tortured, along with eighteen other martyrs, by the fourth-century Roman proconsul Dacian in Zaragoza. Her flesh was flayed by iron nails, her breast opened to expose her heart, and part of her liver was torn out. Miraculously, she survived this ordeal to die a natural death. By the fifteenth century, Engracia's legend had become much more elaborate. She was now a Portuguese princess, who was merely passing through Zaragoza, on the way to meet her fiancé in Roussillon, and the eighteen other martyrs had become her retainers. While in Zaragoza she denounced pagan idol worship and so was apprehended by Dacian, who first killed her retainers, then subjected her to a series of tortures including being dragged through the city bound to the tail of a horse, flagellation, and finally death by driving a spike through her forehead.[1] Engracia's skull with its nail hole was a precious relic of the Benedictine convent of St. Engracia in Zaragoza, built on the site of an oratory dedicated to her since early Christian times. Her popularity was such that many chapels have been dedicated to her in Aragonese churches.

Besides the center effigy of *St. Engracia* and the narrative panel of her capture, several other components of this altarpiece survive. They include two more narratives, *The Flagellation of St. Engracia* in the Museo de Bellas Artes, Bilbao, and the fragmentary *St. Engracia Conducted to Dacian's Palace* in the Museo Colegial, Daroca. The Museo Colegial also houses the *Crucifixion,* which retains part of its enframing *guardapolvos,* and the *banco,* with its five images of *St. Humphrey, St. Prudentius* (?), the *Resurrection, St. Braulius,* and *St. Catherine of Siena.* In the original altarpiece, the Gardner image would have been at the *retablo*'s center, flanked by the narratives (there would have originally been four, symmetrically arranged with two stacked to each side), the *Crucifixion* above the central effigy, and the *banco* below it, extending out the width of the altarpiece.[2] The *Capture of St. Engracia* would have been located in the upper

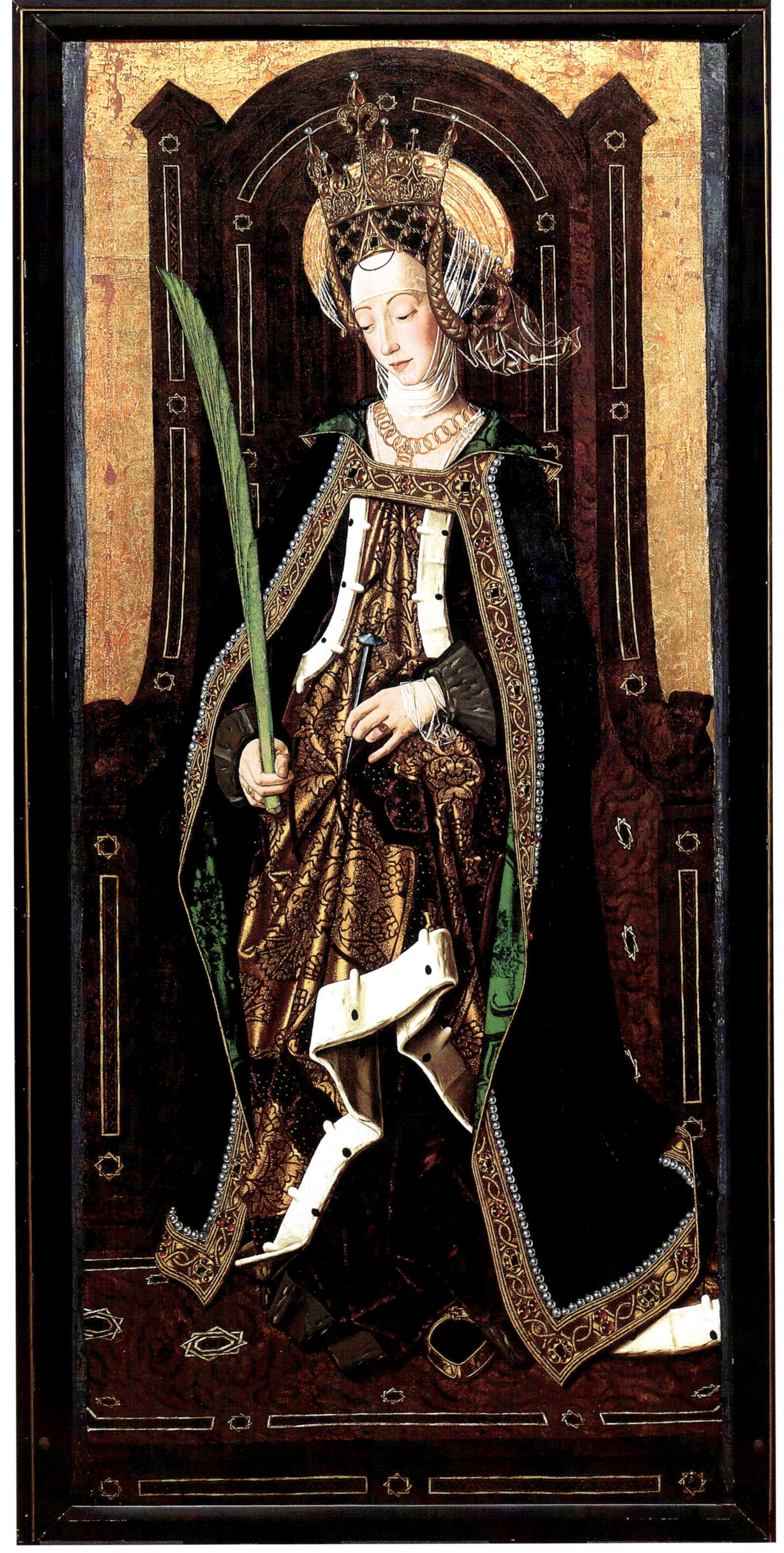

Figure 1-1

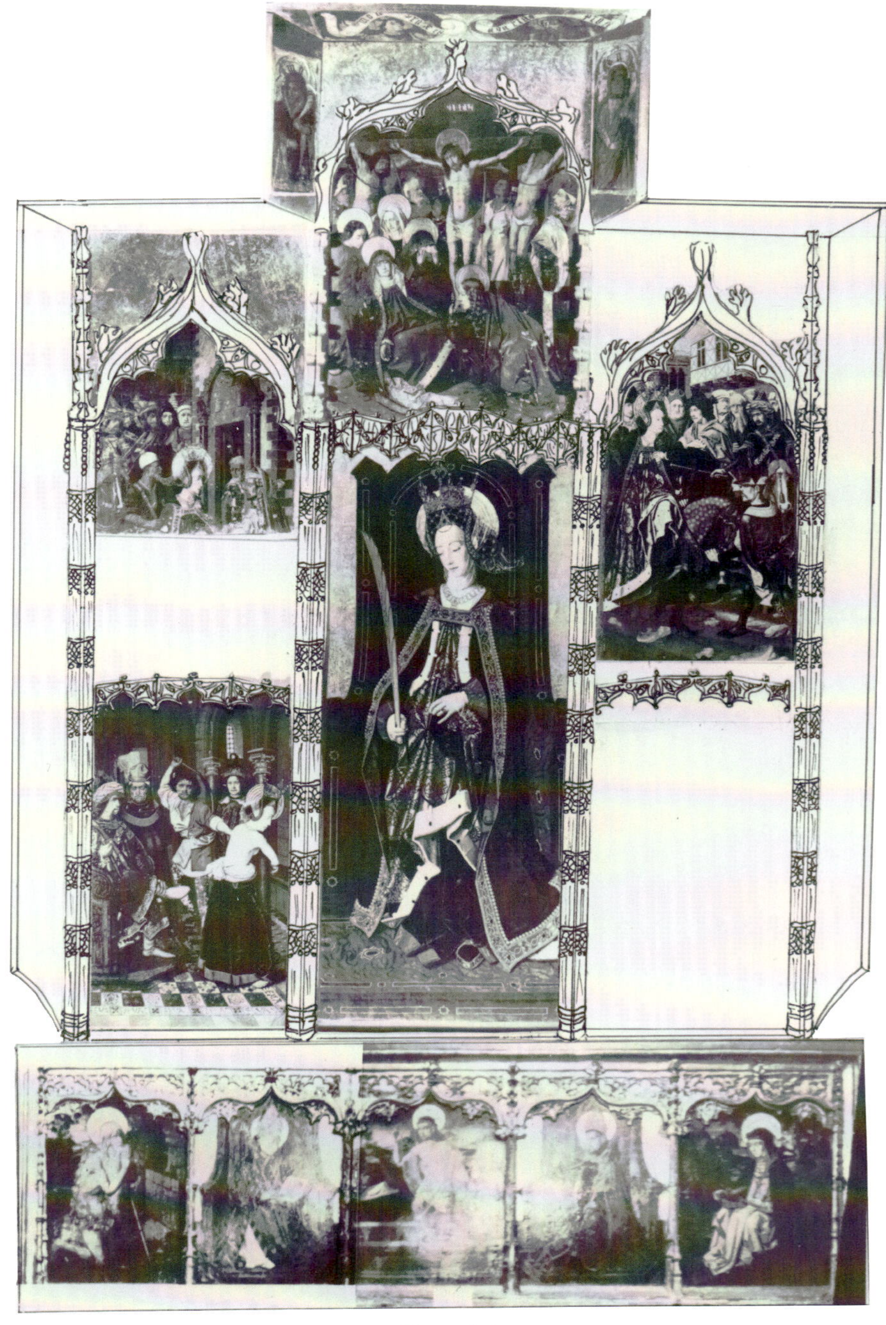

Figure 1-2

tier of narratives; this is evident from its irregularly shaped top, which would have been surrounded by an elaborate frame of Gothic leaves and tracery, called a *chambrana*, typical in Aragonese *retablos* during the fifteenth century (fig. 1-2).[3]

The painter responsible for the *retablo* was Bartolomé de Cárdenas, better known by his nickname Bartolomé Bermejo. According to the inscription on the frame of one of his late works, the *Pietà*, now in the Cathedral Museum of Barcelona, he came from Córdoba; however, no trace of his activity remains there. His mastery of the technique of oil glazing suggests that he may have received some training in Flanders, but Bermejo's career was played out entirely in cities within the Crown of Aragon. He was documented in Valencia in 1468, in the Aragonese cities of Daroca in 1474 and Zaragoza in 1477–1482, and in Barcelona from about 1484 to 1495, with a probable second sojourn in Valencia about 1483–1484.[4]

Given the number of surviving panels from the altarpiece in Daroca, it is fair to suggest that it was probably painted during the artist's documented stay there around 1474, when he was also painting another altarpiece, the *retablo mayor* for the church of Santo Domingo de Silos. It is the contracts for the later *retablo* which also offer a clue to the identity of the church for which the *Retablo of St. Engracia* was intended. The second document referring to Santo Domingo de Silos mentions as a sort of "quality control" some paintings that one of Bermejo's advocates, the merchant Johan de Loperuelo, had painted for a chapel of the church of San Francisco in Daroca.[5] It was common practice for altarpiece contracts to demand that painters paint the contracted work as well as, or perhaps better than, one that they had already completed.[6] The church of San Francisco was destroyed during the exclaustration riots of 1835, and the panel of St. Engracia turned up in the Palacio

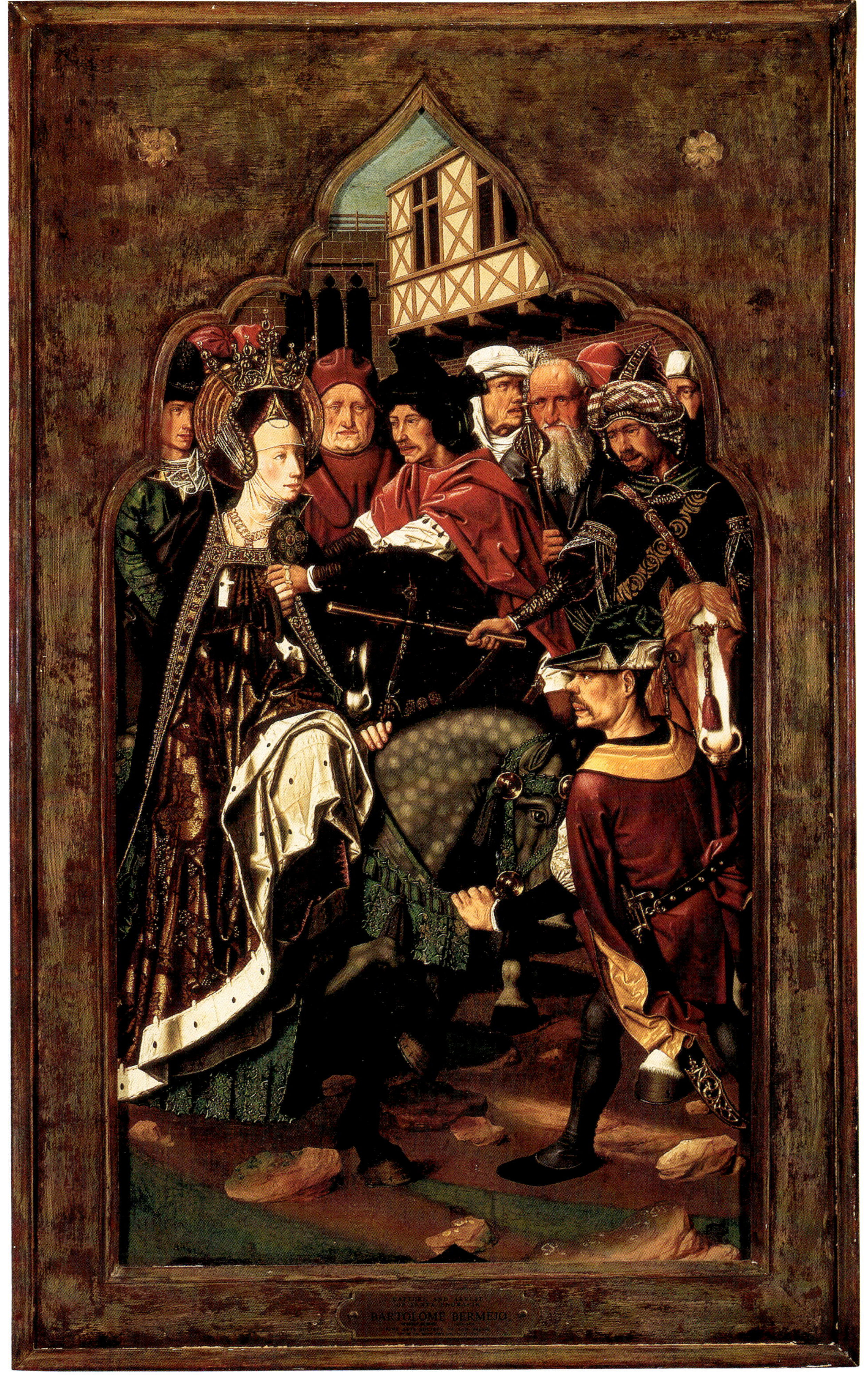

Figure 1-3

de Justicia of Zaragoza at just about that time.[7] The collection of the Museo Colegial in Daroca is made up of paintings which came from now-destroyed churches in Daroca, and the panels from the *Retablo of St. Engracia* in the museum are the peripheral ones, suggesting that when the monastery was destroyed, the altarpiece was broken up (and, judging from the fragmentary *St. Engracia Conducted to Dacian's Palace*, partially mutilated). The three panels now in Boston, San Diego, and Bilbao were sold on the art market, and the remainder were left behind, eventually to be collected when the Museo Colegial was established.[8]

St. Engracia is a typical product of Bermejo's style. The single figure shimmers in her beautiful garments, formally posed with her traditional martyr's palm. The *Capture of St. Engracia* reveals Bermejo's power as a narrator. The melodrama of the scene is accomplished both by gesture and facial expression, with the spectators adding to the air of menace. Following fifteenth-century custom, heroine and villains are portrayed in contemporary dress; thus, Dacian, a Roman pagan, is depicted as the medieval Hispanic Other (the infidel Muslim), while the patrician Engracia wears the court dress of a contemporary noblewoman.[9]

The various textures of clothing, animals, and setting amply demonstrate the painter's mastery of Netherlandish oil glaze technique, somewhat more broadly painted than those of his Flemish contemporaries in order to accommodate the large scale of the *retablo* format. Bermejo adapts this style to Aragonese tastes, retaining the gold ground traditional to the center images of *retablos* and using the *embutido* rings in the haloes, a device particularly favored in this region. The rich but subdued palette of deep wine red, mossy greens, ochres, and deep blues is the painter's own.

1. The legend was recounted by Martín Carrillo, *Historia del glorioso San Valero, obispo de la ciudad de Çaragoça, con los martyrs de San Vicente, Santa Engracia, San Lamberto y los inumerables martyrs naturales patrones y protectores de la Ciudad de Çaragoça,* Zaragoza, 1615, 43ff.

2. Eric Young's reconstruction of the altarpiece (in *Bartolomé Bermejo,* London, Paul Elek, 1975, 120) and that of Juan Francisco Esteban Lorante (*Museo Colegial de Daroca,* Madrid, Servicio Nacional de Información Artística, Arqueológica y Etnológica, 1975, 27) are both erroneous. They postulate too many panels for what had to be a chapel *retablo,* since the *banco* contains no tabernacle in its center, which would have been necessary in a high altar *retablo.* For a more plausible reconstruction, see Judith Berg Sobré, "S. Engracia Revisited," *Fenway Court* (1980), 34–42; a similar reconstruction was proposed independently by Ana Galilea Antón, "Bartolomé Bermejo y el retablo de Santa Engracia. Estado de la cuestión," *Urtekaria Anuario* (1989), 15–31.

3. For the rationale concerning this type of frame, see Berg Sobré, 1980, 36.

4. For a summary of most, but not all, of the relevant documents, see Eric Young, 1975, 17–21. For the second trip to Valencia, see Gianni Rebora, Giacomo Rovera, Giandomenico Bocchiotti, Laboratorio Restauro Nicola de Aramengo, *Bartolomé Bermejo e il trittico di Acqui,* Acqui Terme, 1988, 32–40.

5. See the second contract published by Federico Serrano y Sanz, "Documentos relativos a la pintura en Aragón durante el siglo XV," *Revista de archivos, bibliotecas y museos* 31 (1914), 457–458.

6. See, for example, the contract made between Martín Bernat and the Talavara family for the Cathedral of Tarazona which was to be similar to one already done by Bernat for Zaragoza Cathedral, Serrano y Sanz, 1914, 540–543, 545.

7. J. Fievez, *Catalogue des monuments d'art antique, tableaux anciens, etc. composant les collections de Somzée, II, tableaux anciens,* Brussels, 1904, II, 104.

8. Esteban Lorente, *Museo Colegial de Daroca,* Madrid, Servicio Nacional de Información Artística, Arqueológica y Etnológica (1975), 11–14. For the complete argument for the San Francisco provenance, see Judith Berg Sobré, "Bartolomé de Cárdenas, the Piedat de Johan de Loperuelo, and Painting in Daroca (Aragon)," *The Art Bulletin* 49 (1977), 494–500.

9. It is typical of the ambivalent attitude of Spanish Christians towards Spanish Muslims in this period that Dacian is portrayed as a Muslim, but that Engracia's throne in the central effigy is embellished with the Islamic eight-pointed star, found in many contexts—Christian, Jewish, and Muslim—on the Iberian Peninsula.

Catalogue No. 2

MARTÍN BERNAT

Active in Zaragoza, 1469–1497

St. Blaise Enthroned, ca. 1480
Oil and gold leaf on panel
53 3/4 x 38 1/8 in.
Colnaghi, London and New York

St. Blaise sits on a Gothic throne embellished with dragons on its armrests. He is depicted as a bishop, with a white mitre embellished with jewels, a blue cope with jeweled gold orphreys, a plain pink robe, and scarlet gloves. He holds a crozier, symbol of his rank, and a wool comber's iron, symbol of his martyrdom. Blaise's halo, cope orphreys, crozier, and mitre embellishments are picked out in *embutido,* raised and modeled gesso which is then gilded, a common element in Aragonese *retablos.* A gilded panel forms the background. The floor below him is tiled, and the wall behind the throne is covered with green brocade. This large panel was certainly the center of a *retablo,* which would have been dedicated to St. Blaise and which would have had flanking narratives of scenes from his life, a *Crucifixion* above the central image, and a *banco* with additional saints and the *Dead Christ in His Tomb* at its center.

Blaise was an early Christian bishop, who came from Sebastia in Cappadocia (Armenia) and was martyred there about 313. Of noble birth, he became bishop of Sebastia, but was persecuted by the pagan Roman emperor Licinius. While imprisoned, he miraculously resuscitated a choking boy (and is thus invoked by sufferers of throat diseases). His martyrdom consisted of being flayed with wool comber's irons and then being beheaded. Blaise was quite popular in Aragon, and a substantial number of *retablos* are dedicated to him.[1] Some may have been commissioned in thanks because the donor suffered from a throat ailment, but it is more likely that the majority bore this dedication because Blaise, with his wool comber's irons, was the patron saint of many workers such as carders, combers, and beaters in the wool industry, one of the most important components of Aragon's economy.

The master responsible for this panel was Martín Bernat.[2] Bernat headed one of the most prolific workshops in Zaragoza during the last quarter of the fifteenth century. His family came from the lower nobility, unusual for a painter in this period, for documents refer to him as *scudero* (squire or nobleman) or *infanzón* (member of the lower nobility).[3] His rank certainly never came in conflict with his career, for Bernat became an exemplary craftsman and successful businessman in his trade, producing numerous large *retablos* for churches in Zaragoza as well as towns surrounding it and as far away as Barbastro, north of Huesca. As well as painting *retablos* on his own, Bernat collaborated with various painters during his career, including Bartolomé Bermejo (1477–1479), Miguel Ximénez (1482–1496), and the Castilian painter Hernando del Rincón (1491).[4] Of the three, the one who had the strongest impact on him was Bermejo. In 1477, Bernat agreed to complete Bermejo's unfinished high altar *retablo* dedicated to Santo Domingo de Silos for the parish church of the same name in Daroca (though Bermejo apparently subsequently completed it himself).[5] Bermejo had by then moved from Daroca to Zaragoza, and in 1479 contracted to collaborate with Bernat for a *retablo* for the St. Cristina chapel in the church of El Pilar. The relationship between the two painters during this period was apparently close: Bermejo was excommunicated for his failure to complete the Daroca *retablo,* and Bernat was acting as his guarantor. But if Bernat was acting as Bermejo's legal supporter, he received a great deal from him in turn: the elements of his painting style.

It is not clear if Bernat actually ever trained with Bermejo, but he was certainly familiar with works that Bermejo produced in Daroca, where he resided at least from 1474 until some time before 1477. This can be seen directly in the *St. Blaise,* which is clearly based on Bermejo's center panel for the *retablo mayor* of Santo Domingo de Silos (fig. 2-2), which shows that saint enthroned in a similar manner.[6] Bermejo derived his own composition from earlier Aragonese images of enthroned bishop saints, such as the *St. Nicholas* in the church of Sts. Justa and Rufina in Maluenda, but in doing so, he redefined the prototype. His rendition is extremely subtle, similar in technique to the contemporaneous *St. Engracia* also in this exhibition, down to the eight-pointed Mudéjar stars that embellish the throne.

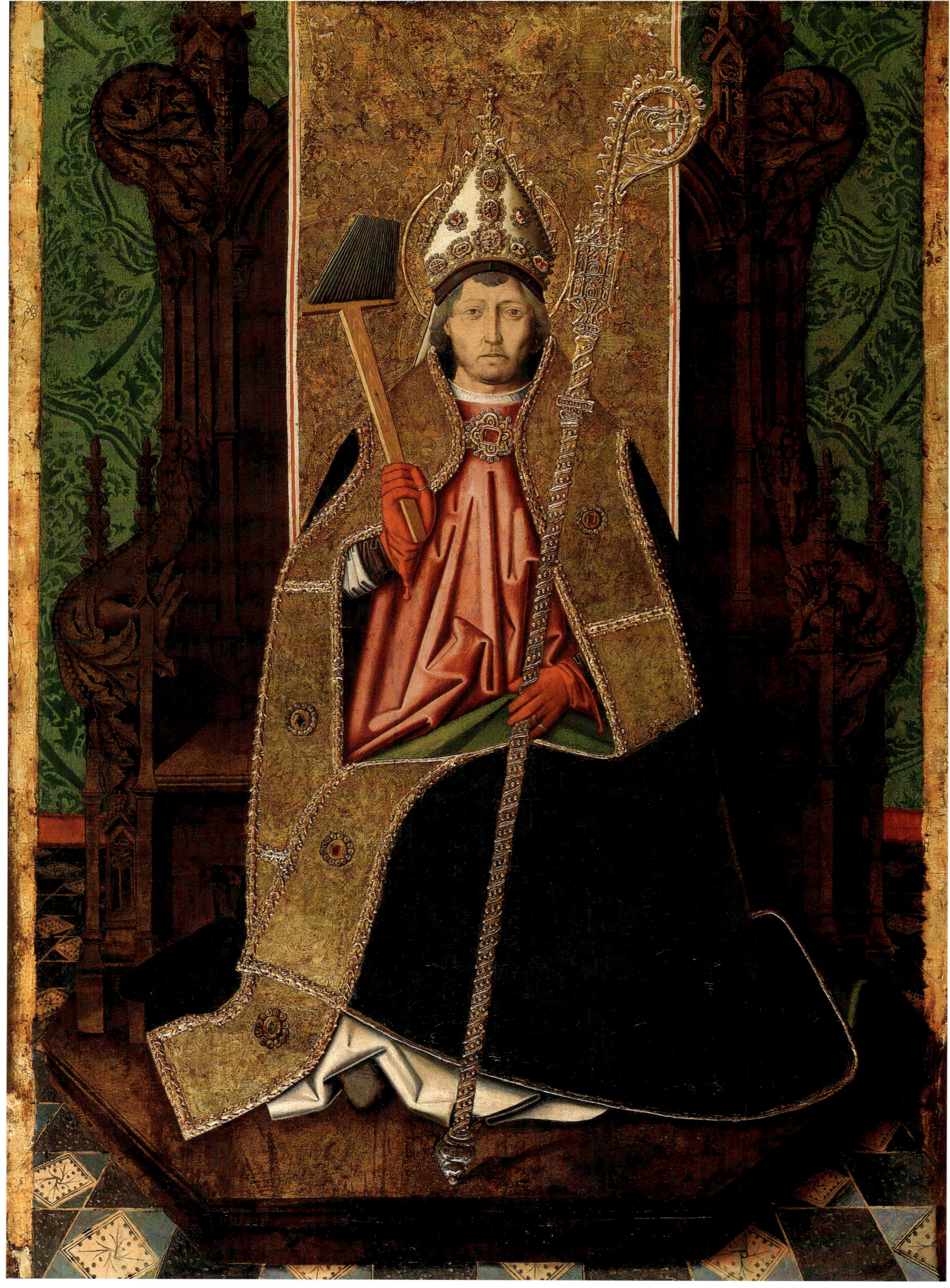

Figure 2-1

Bernat's version, though similar in color scheme, is harder and less detailed, features larger patterns on fabrics and hangings, and uses *embutido* ornamentation; all of these traits are typical of later-fifteenth-century Aragonese painting.

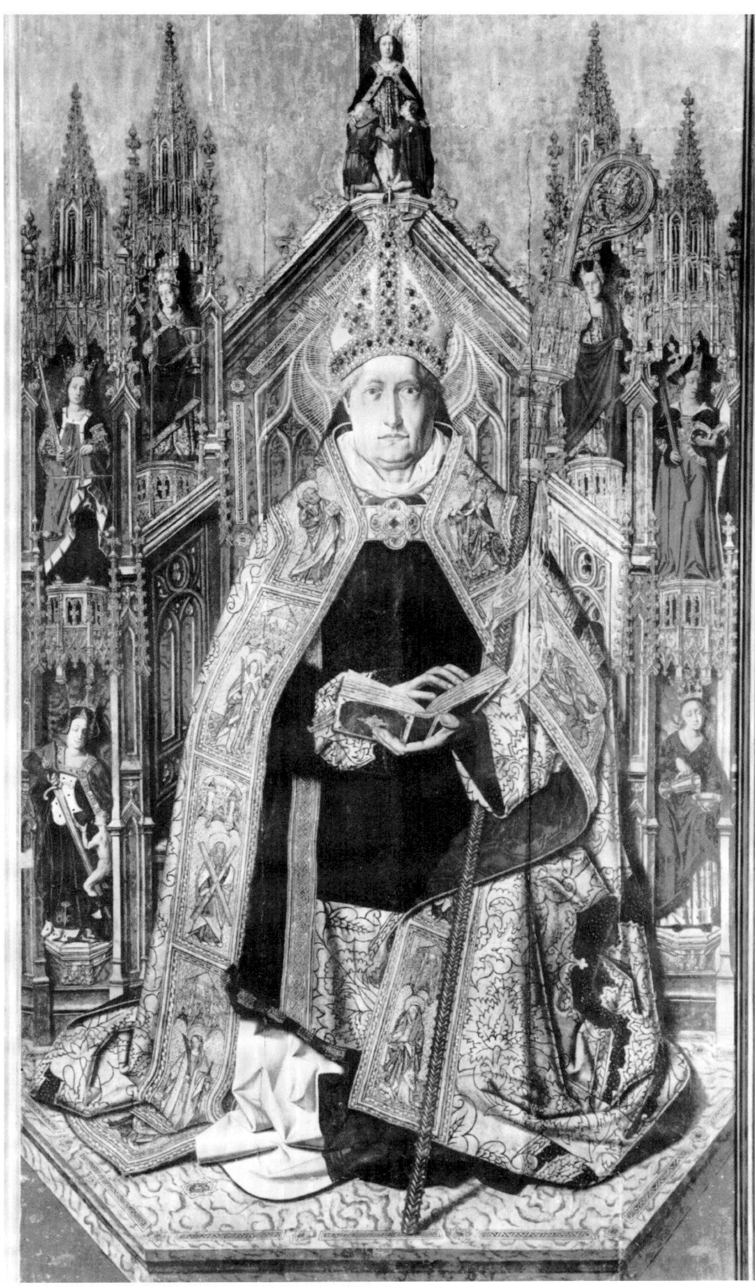

Figure 2-2

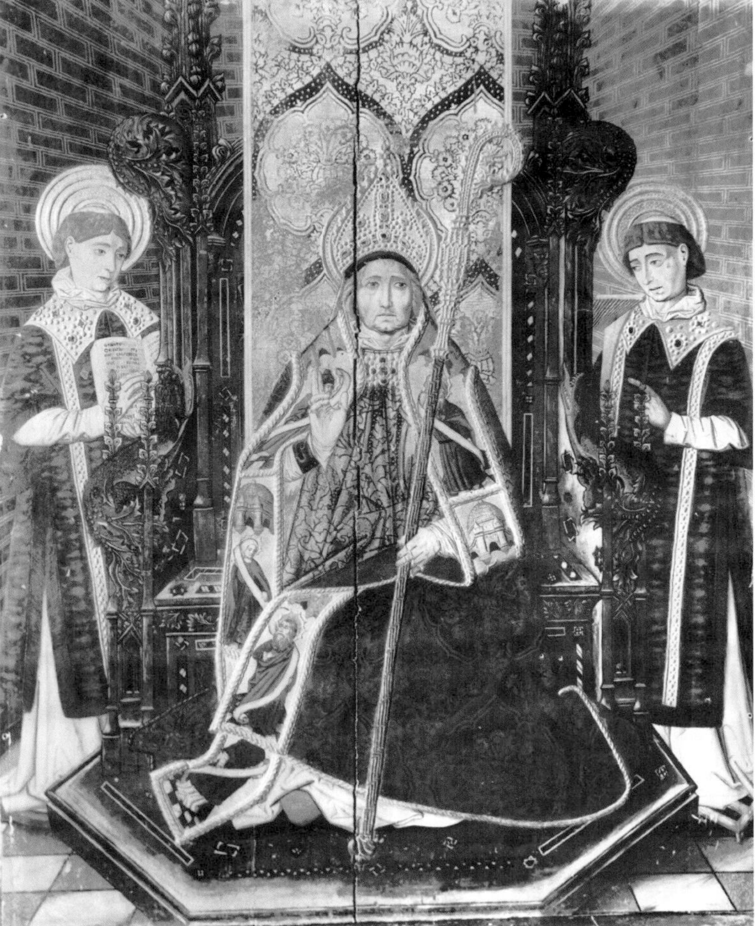

Figure 2-3

Bernat evidently became attached to this composition, for he repeated it many times; other versions of *St. Blaise*, with minor variations, are found in the center of *retablos* he and his shop made for the parish church of Lécera (fig. 2-3), one for an unknown destination that was formerly in the Parcent collection, Madrid, and another for the parish church of Piedratajada.[7] But he went even further: He used the same composition, with appropriate modifications in attributes, settings, and subsidiary figures, to represent other saints. These include St. Martin in two versions, one in the Hispanic Society of America, the other, replete with beggar, saintly knight, and St. Stephen in a *retablo* from Lascuarre; St. Victorian, this time accompanied by Sts. Gaudiosus and Nazarius, in the Cathedral of Barbastro; and St. Augustine, now in the Museum of Dijon.

Such reuse of compositions from a master cartoon was approved practice during the fifteenth century; contracts frequently specify such borrowing. Stylistic borrowing was likewise encouraged in an era when painting was a corporate enterprise and painters were contractors.[8] Nevertheless, it is clear that Bermejo was the Bach or Shakespeare of his time, taking older compositions or forms and making definitive restatements of them which became archetypes, while Bernat was more of a Vivaldi or Marlowe, producing many excellent works, but often given to formula.

1. The number of surviving *retablos* or portions of Aragonese *retablos* dedicated to St. Blaise are too numerous to mention. For a list of them, see the catalogue in José Gudiol Ricart, *Pintura medieval in Aragón,* Zaragoza, Institución Fernando el Católico, 1971, 71–87.

2. Chandler R. Post (*A History of Spanish Painting,* VIII, Cambridge, Mass., 1941, 155) attributed the work to the Alfajarín Master, who was subsequently identified by José Gudiol Ricart as Martín Bernat (*Ars Hispaniae IX: Pintura Gótica,* Madrid, Editorial Plus Ultra, 1955, 306).

3. See, for example, Serrano y Sanz, "Documentos relativos a la pintura en Aragon durante el siglo XV," *Revista de archivos, bibliotecas y museos* 35 (1916), 481–482.

4. See María del Carmen Lacarra Ducay, "Sobre dibujos preparatorios para retablos de pintores aragoneses del siglo XV," *Anuario de estudios medievales,* Barcelona, 1983, 560, for a thumbnail biography of Bernat (whom she calls Bernart).

5. See Judith Berg Sobré, *Bartolomé de Cárdenas, el Bermejo,* New York, International Scholars Publications, in press, for a detailed accounting of the relationship of Bermejo and Bernat.

6. See the comparison made by Donald Garstang, *Colnaghi: Master Paintings,* London, 1994, 26–29.

7. The *retablo* for Piedratajada bore a triple dedication to Sts. Sebastian, Christopher, and Blaise. Here Sebastian was in the center, for the church of Piedratajada is dedicated to him.

8. See, for example, the case of Gonçal Peris de Sarrià's *St. Lucy,* fig. 5-1.

Catalogue No. 3

FRANCESC COMES

Active in Mallorca, 1392–1415

The Virgin and Child, Sts. George, Martin, and Anthony Abbot, ca. 1395

Tempera and gold leaf on panel

29 9/16 x 45 1/8 in.

Isabella Stewart Gardner Museum, Boston

P16e16

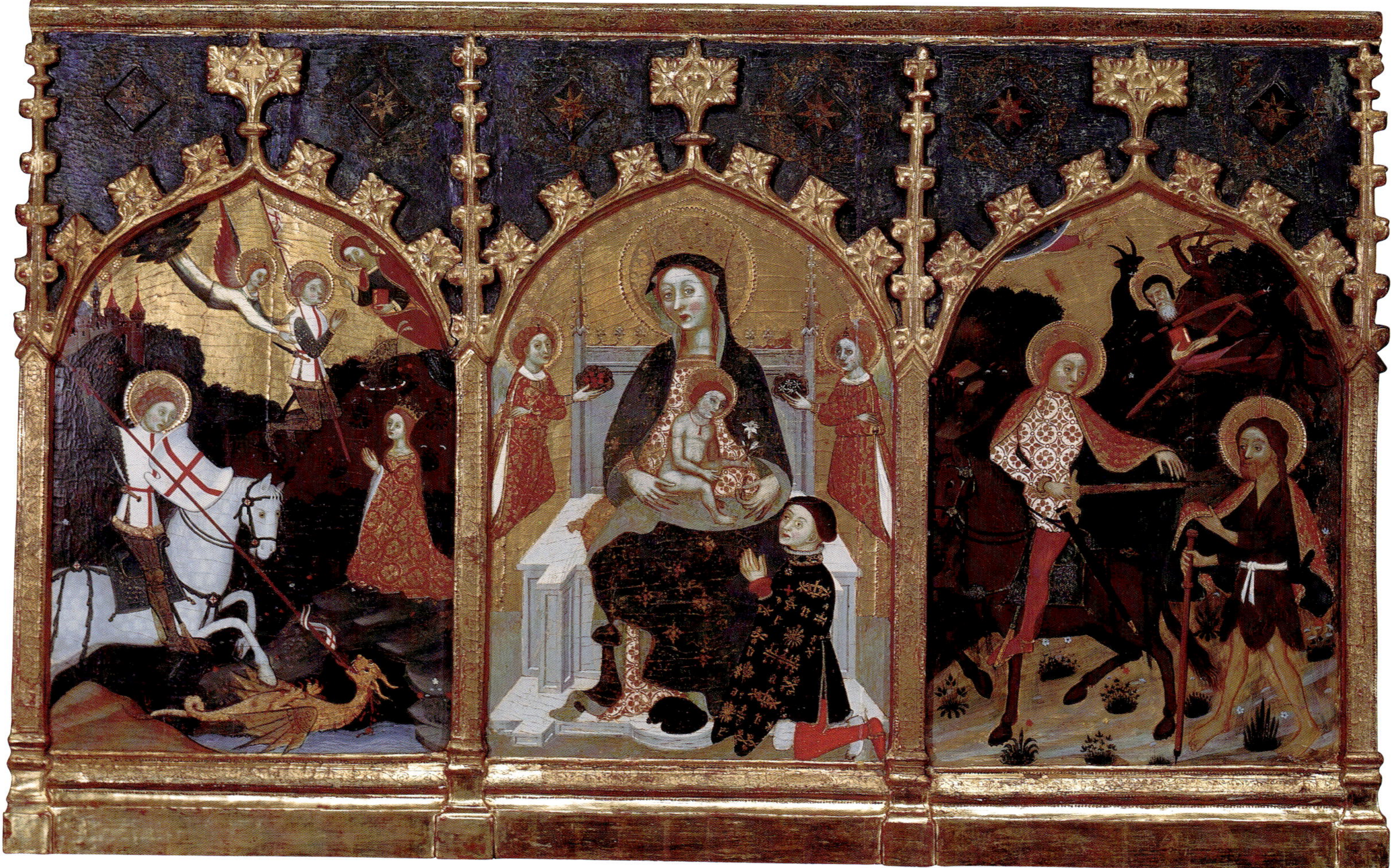

Figure 3-1

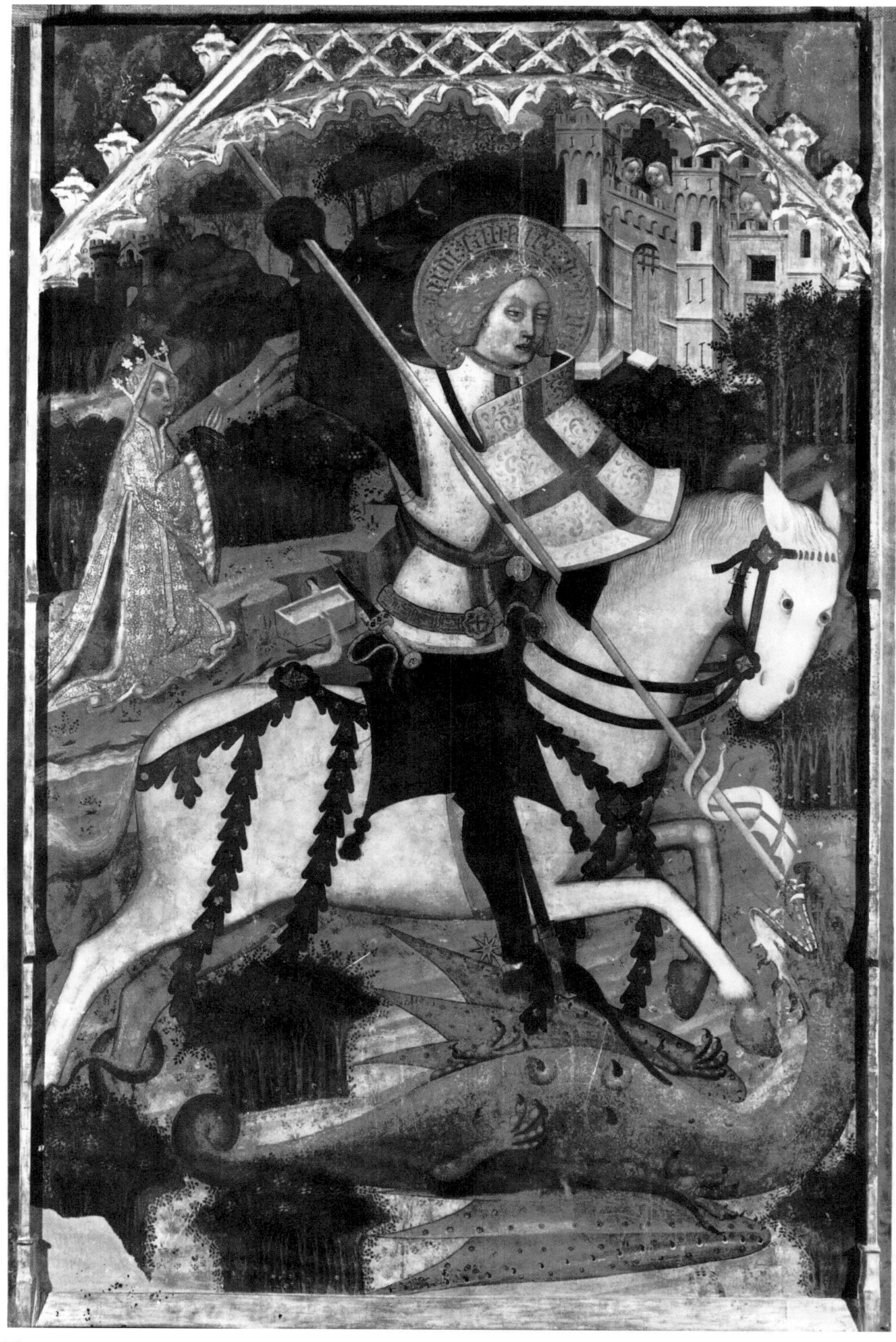

Figure 3-2

The work consists of three fixed compartments surrounded by frames of Gothic tracery and pinnacles. All are the same size. In the center is the Virgin Mary enthroned with the Christ Child; she is flanked by two angels who offer her flowers while a donor kneels at her feet. In the left compartment, St. George slays the dragon while the princess looks on. George appears again in the background, where an angel presents him to Christ. This latter incident occurred when George was imprisoned (and awaiting martyrdom) during the anti-Christian campaign of the Emperor Diocletian. In the right compartment, St. Martin divides his cloak with a beggar in the foreground, while in the background is the temptation of St. Anthony by a collection of demons.

If it is complete, the format of this triptych is unusual in the art of the Crown of Aragon. Triptychs, when found on the Iberian Peninsula, usually are small in size and have folding wings; they were portable altarpieces used for private devotion. The type of framing used here, and the fixed nature of the three scenes on a single panel only a little over two feet high, suggest instead a *banco,* the predella-like strip of paintings found at the very bottom of Hispanic *retablos. Bancos* normally had more than two scenes flanking their center compartments, but it appears from the upper molding that the original panel perhaps extended further to either side, and so there may have been additional compartments which have now been lost. There is no encasing frame around the whole panel, which was customary in *banco* construction, but it might have been removed. *Bancos* usually had the eucharistic theme of the *Dead Christ in His Tomb* in their center; however, the Virgin Mary might occasionally occupy this position, depending on the subject matter of the body of the *retablo.* This variability is particularly common in Mallorcan painting, where the *retablos* have greater variation in their format and layout than elsewhere in the Crown of Aragon, perhaps because of the island location.[1]

For reasons of style and composition, this work has been attributed to Francesc Comes, a painter documented to have been working on the island of Mallorca from 1392 to 1415.[2] Comes painted a number of *retablos* during this career, the center panel of one of which, depicting *St. George Killing the Dragon* (from the convent of Sant Francesc, Inca, and now in the Museo de Mallorca in Palma de Mallorca), replicates on a grand scale the left panel of the triptych. In spite of its small size, the Palma panel (fig. 3-2) is more subtly painted. George is identified by an inscription in his halo, and the princess, who is placed to the left of George in this version, wears a much finer brocaded gown. A castle is in the background.[3] The general style of both panels conforms to the painting style of late-fourteenth-century Mallorca, which has relationships both to Catalan painting of the period (such as the work of Jaime and Pere Serra) and to Italian painting of the late trecento—not surprisingly considering the fact that the Balearic Islands, of which Mallorca is a part, had strong commercial ties both to the mainland of the Crown of Aragon and to Italy.

The donor figure in the *Virgin and Child* compartment wears a gold-embroidered black doublet comprising a number of different devices, but the most prominent is a double crown, which has been identified with the *corona doble* of Aragon, a device created by the Aragonese king Juan I in 1392 and associated with the last kings of the original ruling house of the Crown of Aragon.[4] It has been suggested that the donor might be the king himself.[5] Since Comes painted two portraits of English royalty for King Juan in 1395, it is possible that in this triptych (whatever its true function) he was enjoying royal patronage a second time.[6]

1. See Judith Berg Sobré, *Behind the Altar Table,* Columbia, Mo., University of Missouri Press, 1989, 119–132.

2. It was believed that the painter Francesc Comes, documented in Valencia from 1380 until 1400, was identifiable with the Francesc Comes active on Mallorca, see Judith Berg Sobré, "A Triptych by Francesc Comes," *Fenway Court* (1969), 11–12. However, Pere Llompart (*La Pintura Medieval Mallorquina,* I, Palma de Mallorca, Luis Ripoll, 1977, 70) has pointed out that the Valencian Francesc Comes is mentioned in a document of 1400 as being deceased at that time (this document is reproduced in Lluís Cerveró Gomis, "Pintores valentinos, su cronología y documentación," *Archivo de arte valenciano* 43 [1971], 28). We are, therefore, dealing with two different painters of the same name.

3. See Berg Sobré, 1969, 10. The attribution was also made independently by Chandler R. Post (*A History of Spanish Painting,* XI, Cambridge, Mass., 1958, 384) though he called the painter the Inca Master.

4. A. Van de Put, "A Primitive at Boston and the Double Crown of Aragon," *Art in America* 20 (1932), 51–59. Van de Put makes an exhaustive analysis of the heraldry on the donor's coat and suggests that the donor is Fadrich, bastard son of Martin the Younger, king of Sicily.

5. Martí de Riquer (*Bernat Metge, obras completas,* Barcelona, 1959, 13) mentions a description of Juan by Bernat Metge, his secretary, in which he is wearing a robe decorated with the *corona doble,* though the velvet was red instead of black. In a letter in the Gardner Museum files (April 11, 1959), Riquer suggests that the work could have been ordered when Juan I resided in Mallorca during the summer of 1395, when he was fleeing a plague outbreak on the mainland.

6. For the document concerning the royal portraits, see Llompart, 1977, 110–111.

Catalogue No. 4

PERE GARCÍA DE BENABARRE

Active in Catalonia and eastern Aragon, 1445–1483

St. Michael, after 1461

Tempera and gold leaf on panel
72 x 56 in.
Isabella Stewart Gardner Museum, Boston
P19s7

St. Michael appears simultaneously in his two most famous roles: as weigher of souls and vanquisher of the dragon/demon. Clad in armor embellished with *embutido* studs, he sits on a parapet-backed throne painted in faulty perspective so that he actually appears to squat, with a strip of brocade behind him. To his right, an angel embraces a blessed soul, while the demon/dragon (who resembles a modern science-fiction space alien) lies nearly prone beneath his feet, yet still manages to claim the damned soul in the scale to Michael's left. The ground behind the throne is gilded with a thistle pattern modeled in *embutido*, and the floor below is tiled.

This panel is extremely large—more than six feet in height and four-and-a-half feet in width, and it is astounding to realize that this is merely a *side* panel of a colossal *retablo mayor,* dedicated to St. John the Baptist. Aside from a *St. Jerome* (Museu d'Art de Catalunya, Barcelona) (fig. 4-2), all of the other surviving panels deal with episodes from St. John's life. They include *The Annunciation of John's Birth to Zacharias* (Milà collection, Barcelona), *The Visitation* (private collection, Seville), *The Birth of John the Baptist, The Inscription of John's Name, The Baptism of Christ, The Feast of Herod* (fig. 4-3), and *The Decapitation of John the Baptist* (all in the Museu d'Art de Catalunya).[1] All of the panels are large and of similar dimensions (the *St. Michael* is slightly lower and wider than the others), and all must have constituted lateral narratives around a central image of John, painted or sculpted, though it is not clear how *St. Michael* and *St. Jerome* fit into the lateral scheme.[2] The other standard *retablo* components—*Crucifixion*, central effigy, *banco,* tabernacle, and *guardapolvos*—are all missing.

Though the immediate provenance of these panels was the parish church of Benavent, near Huesca in Aragon, the altarpiece was commissioned for and originally placed behind the high altar of the church of Sant Joan del Mercat in the Catalan city of Lleida, and it doubtless filled up the entire apse. Though the church of Sant Joan del Mercat is now destroyed, it is not clear when these panels were moved to Benavent.[3]

The altarpiece is largely the work of Pere García, active from 1445 until 1483.[4] Early writers dealing with this master called him Pere García de Benabarre, since he signed a panel of the *Virgin and Child* from the parish church of Bellcaire de Noguera in this manner.[5] It was therefore assumed that he came from Benabarre, in Aragon. However, no extant documentation places him there.[6] The earliest mention of Pere García finds him in Zaragoza in 1445, where he served as a witness to an apprenticeship contract with the Aragonese painter Blasco de Grañén. Later in that year, he was in Huesca. In 1452, he signed a five-year contract with the widow and son of Bernat Martorell in Barcelona to finish works left pending after Martorell's death. Since the agreement states that he would be given furnished quarters in the Martorell family home, it is evident that García was moving in from elsewhere. Martorell was the leading master of his generation in Barcelona, and his heirs had quarreled with Miquel Nadal, the painter whom he had designated to take over his establishment. Though García was a second choice, the post was still a plum, and it speaks to his reputation among his peers as a painter. It is not clear why he did not remain in Barcelona, but in 1473, he was practicing his craft in Lleida, and it is probable that the *Retablo of St. John the Baptist* dates from this period, since Sant Joan del Mercat was located there. His career appears to have ended in the Aragonese city of Barbastro, where he lived and worked from 1481 to 1496.

So where does Benabarre fit in? There are some works by Pere García which were painted in and around Benabarre, including four panels from a *retablo* dedicated to the Virgin still in that city. The style of those works has been considered early, and so scholars tend to maintain

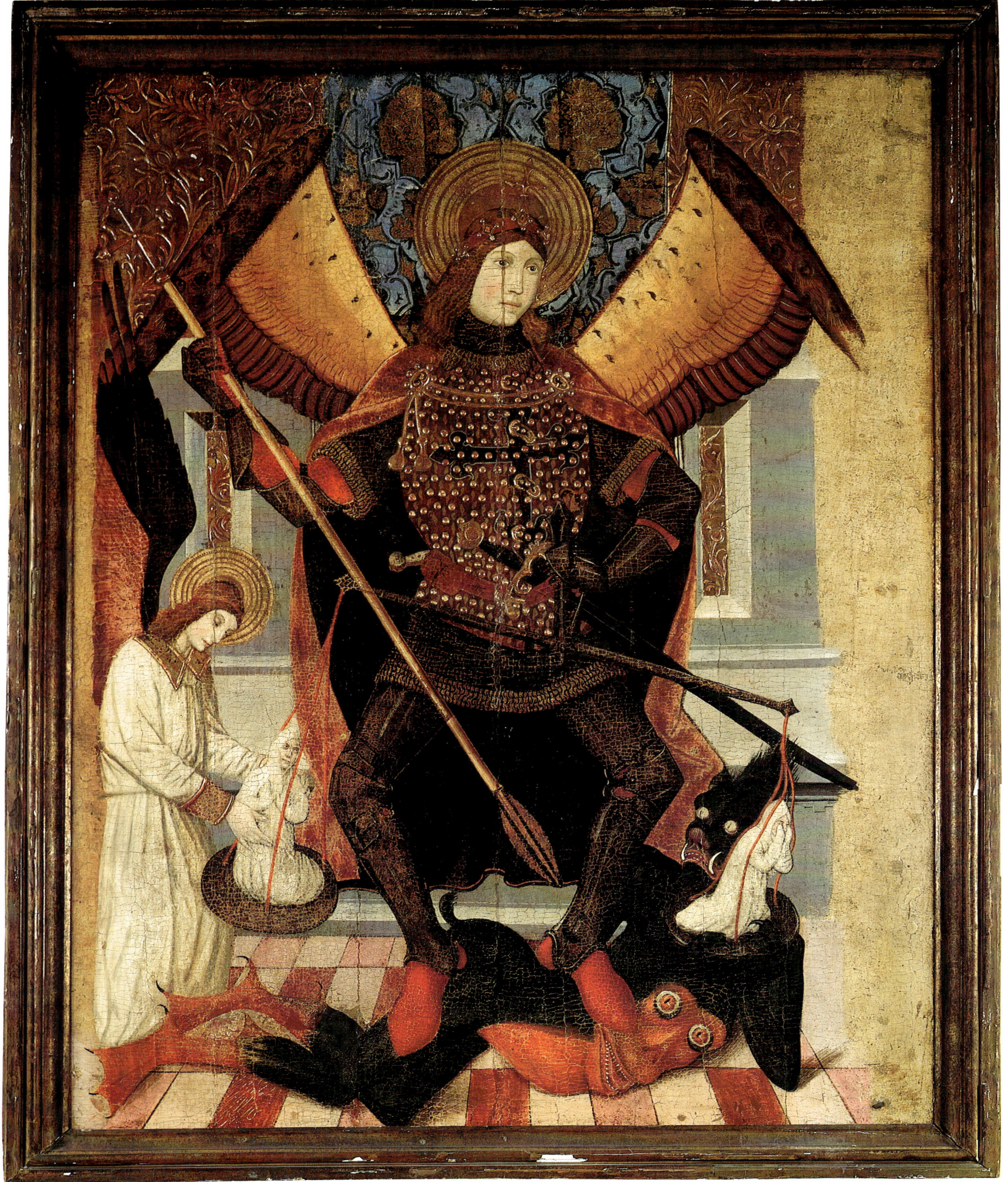

Figure 4-1

that he spent the earliest part of his career in Benabarre (ca. 1450–1455) before he turned up in Zaragoza.[7]

Art historians generally see the influence of the Catalan painter Jaume Huguet in the figural types and manner of execution in Pere García's work.[8] Huguet was the foremost master of his day in Barcelona, the real inheritor of Bernat Martorell's artistic mantle, and it is obvious that Pere García

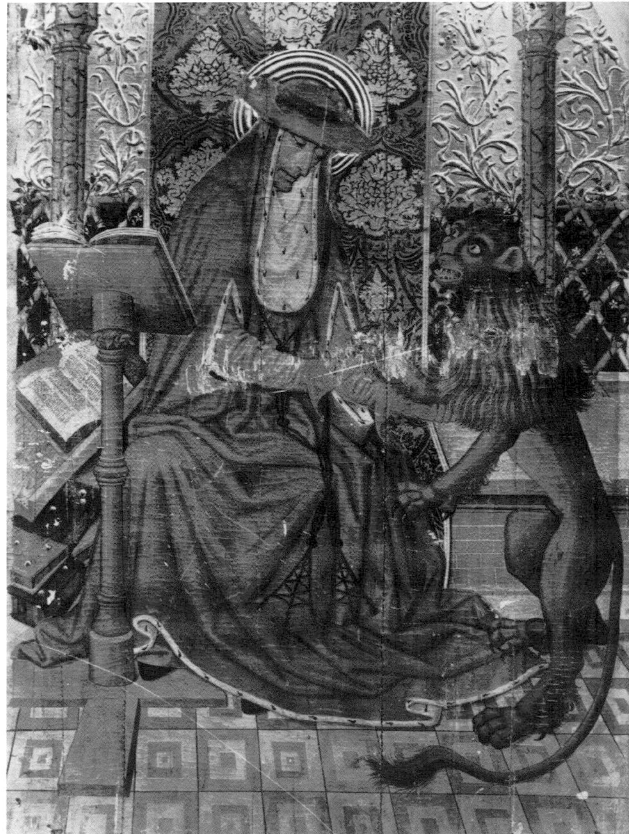

Figure 4-2

is a related, though decidedly less distinguished talent. It should be pointed out, however, that Pere García and Jaume Huguet were almost exact contemporaries (Huguet was still a minor in 1437 and died in 1492). It is possible that both derived something of their styles from Bernat Martorell, and both were probably active in Zaragoza relatively early in their careers, so their professional developments may simply have taken parallel courses. Pere García's itinerant operations apparently included extensive workshops. Not only did the anonymous Master of Viella work on *retablos* produced in his shop, but Pere García probably trained another, more rustic master, Pere Espalargues, who subsequently filled parish churches in northern Catalan towns with crudely executed altarpieces that still hark back to Pere García models.

The *St. Michael* is one of the finer productions from Pere García's workshop, and one upon which he probably lavished his personal attention, but the same cannot be said for other parts of the *retablo*. However, it must be remembered that *retablos* were painted on a grand, rather than an intimate scale; *retablos mayores* were meant to be seen from a distance by the parishioners, and they were surrounded by elaborate gilt frames. For such huge works, bright colors and glittering gilded grounds and ornaments helped make the stories they told intelligible to those attending Mass. In such a context, the subtleties of master and workshop were seldom noticed, so Pere García was simply being true to the common practice of the time.[9]

1. All the panels from this altarpiece still in Spain are illustrated and inventoried in Santiago Alcolea Blanch and José Gudiol Ricart, *Pintura gótica catalana*, Barcelona, Edicions Polígrafa, 1987, 187–188 and 440–441, figs. 926–933.

2. Spanish *retablos* sometimes had triple dedications, and therefore three main effigies, but if this altarpiece were one of these, the *St. Jerome* and the *St. Michael* would have had to have been larger in scale than the narratives.

3. It is quite possible that they were moved at an earlier date than the church's destruction. In several other cases, a *retablo*, removed from its altar in one church due to replacement or demolition, was recycled to another, the most famous being the *retablo mayor* of León Cathedral. See F. J. Sánchez Cantón, *Maestre Nicolas Frances*, Madrid, Instituto Diego Velázquez, 1964, 14–15.

4. Alcolea Blanch and Gudiol Ricart, 1987, 189; see the intervention of a second master, probably a shop collaborator, called the Master of Viella, in some of the panels dealing with the life of St. John.

5. Chandler R. Post, *A History of Spanish Painting* VII, Cambridge, Mass., 1938, 265.

6. The compendium of documentation and their sources are found in Alcolea Blanch and Gudiol Ricart, 1987, 186.

7. Ibid., 187.

8. Ibid. The authors see Huguet's influence early, and they suggest that contact came during Huguet's early activity in Zaragoza. Post (1938, 266) believes that the influence is somewhat more remote.

9. It should be noted, however, that the interventions of the master in individual panels of *retablos* are often found in the lowest sections of the altarpiece—and are, therefore, closer to the viewer. These sections would include the principal effigy, *banco* panels, and the lowest narratives, and this may be a clue to the placement of the *St. Michael* within the *retablo.*

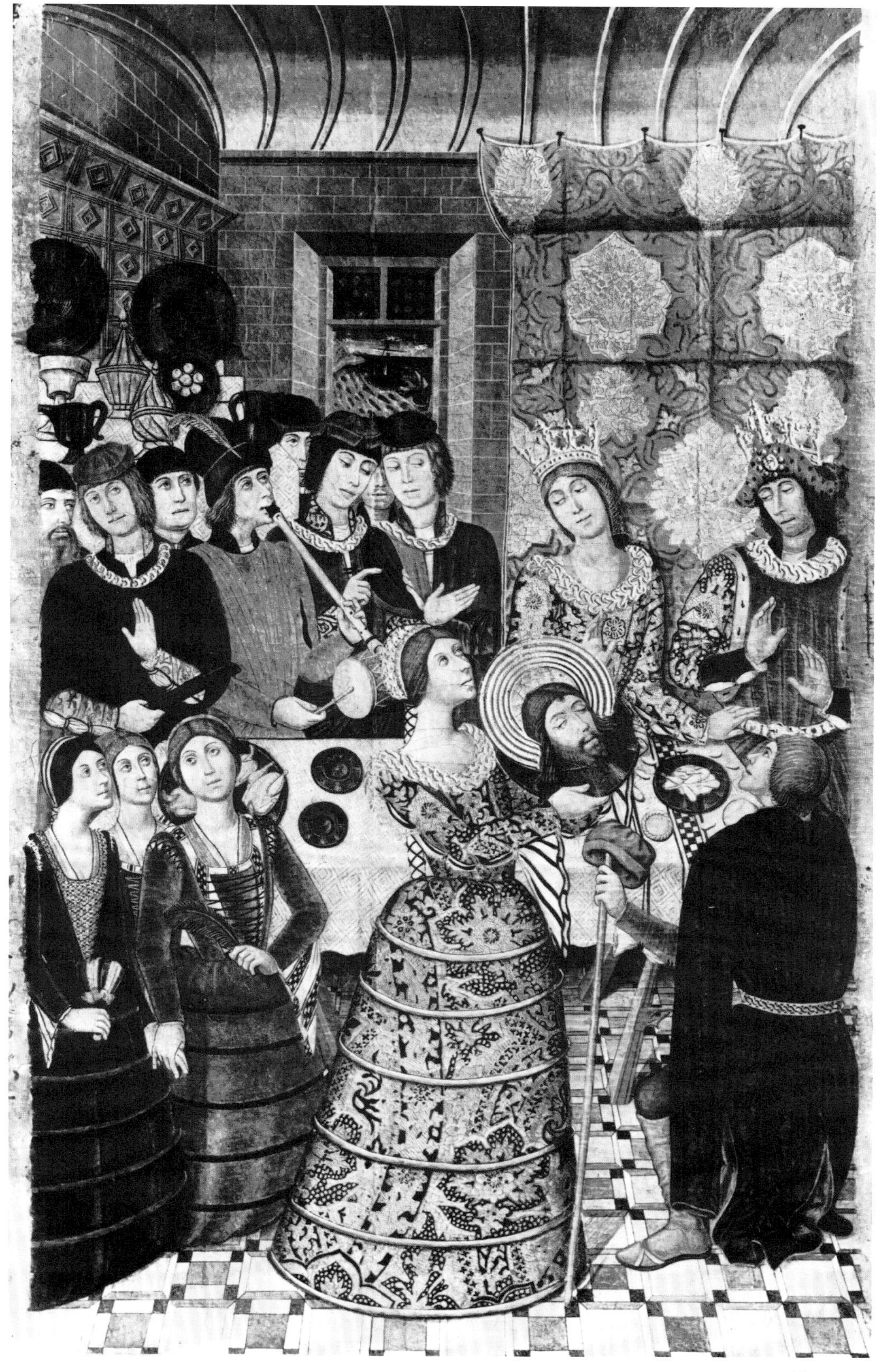

Figure 4-3

Catalogue No. 5

GONÇAL PERIS DE SARRIÀ

Active in Valencia, 1380–1451

St. Lucy, ca. 1425
Egg tempera and some oil on conifer panel
56 1/8 x 36 5/8 in.
Williams College Museum of Art
Gift of Karl E. Weston, Class of 1896, in memory of Ruth Sabin Weston
54.2

St. Lucy stands on a now-eroded brocaded carpet before a thronelike structure, which is in turn placed in front of a gold ground with a floral and mock-Islamic punched design at its side borders. Lucy's halo is adorned with a similar floral panel. The saint is blond and she wears a delicately brocaded robe and a blue mantle lined with orange. In her right hand she holds a martyr's palm; in her left, a salver with her attribute, her eyes.

Lucy was an early Christian virgin martyred in Sicily when she vowed to give away all her wealth and renounce her pagan fiancé, the Roman consul Paschasius, after her mother was miraculously cured of a blood disease at the tomb of St. Agatha. Though her tortures were many, they had nothing to do with her eyes; death came from a sword-thrust after suffering ordeals by fire and burning pitch. The legend of Lucy's plucking out her eyes to defy Paschasius (or having them plucked out by him) was a later medieval addition to her tale; it probably has something to do with her name, Lucy or Lucia having the same root as the Latin *lux* ("light") and *lucifer* ("light-bearing"). By the fifteenth century, Lucy was invariably depicted in European painting holding a set of eyes on a plate.

This panel was originally the center of a *retablo* dedicated to St. Lucy. None of the narrative panels survives, but the provenance of this panel is known to have been the Convent of St. Claire in the Andalusian city of Ubeda.[1] Another panel, an *Annunciation,* in a very similar style exists in the Museu d'Art de Catalunya in Barcelona; it also probably came from Ubeda.[2] It is somewhat wider than the *St. Lucy* (90 cm for the former, 83.8 cm for the latter); however, allowing for possible cutting of the sides of the panels and framing elements, it is possible to postulate (with some reservations) that the *Annunciation* may have occupied a position above *St. Lucy* in the *retablo.*

We do not know whether the *Retablo of St. Lucy* was for a high altar or for a chapel, but its resemblance to another *retablo*, that of *St. Barbara* from Puertomingalvo in Aragon, now in the Museu d'Art de Catalunya (fig. 5-2), gives an approximate idea about its appearance. The *Retablo of St. Barbara* features the central effigy of the saint flanked by eight narratives (in groups of two) and surmounted by *Christ on the Cross.* Each of these panels is separated from the others by a gilded frame, with pinnacles above the top elements. The entire *retablo* excluding the *banco* is surrounded by *guardapolvos*, or dust-guards, decorated strips of wood slightly tilted inward to protect the altarpiece, and embellished with large rosettes in relief and coats of arms. Below is the *banco*, a horizontal strip of seven images, which would have rested upon the altar table or just behind it. Four virgin martyrs occupy the outer compartments, while the lamenting Virgin Mary and John the Evangelist flank a now-blank space that would have been occupied by the *Dead Christ in His Tomb*, a eucharistic reference found in virtually all *retablos* from this period in the Crown of Aragon.

We can speak of the similarity of the configuration of *St. Lucy's retablo* to that of *St. Barbara* because the two central effigies are not only the same size but are virtually identical except for attributes (Barbara holds her identifying tower instead of a plate with eyes). When the *St. Lucy* was recently restored, it was noted that outlines of the figure were incised into the gesso layer.[3] Similar lines were incised into the *St. Barbara*, suggesting that a common cartoon was used for both, the attributes being changed to suit the saint.

Such shortcuts reveal something of the workshop practices in early-fifteenth-century Spain. Both pieces came from the workshop of Gonçal Peris de Sarrià, a prolific painter active in the city of Valencia during the first half of the fifteenth century. Peris is known to have repeated a figure in another instance: in two images of St. John the Baptist, one the center of a *retablo* from Ródenas (Aragon), the other from Burgo de Osma (Castile).

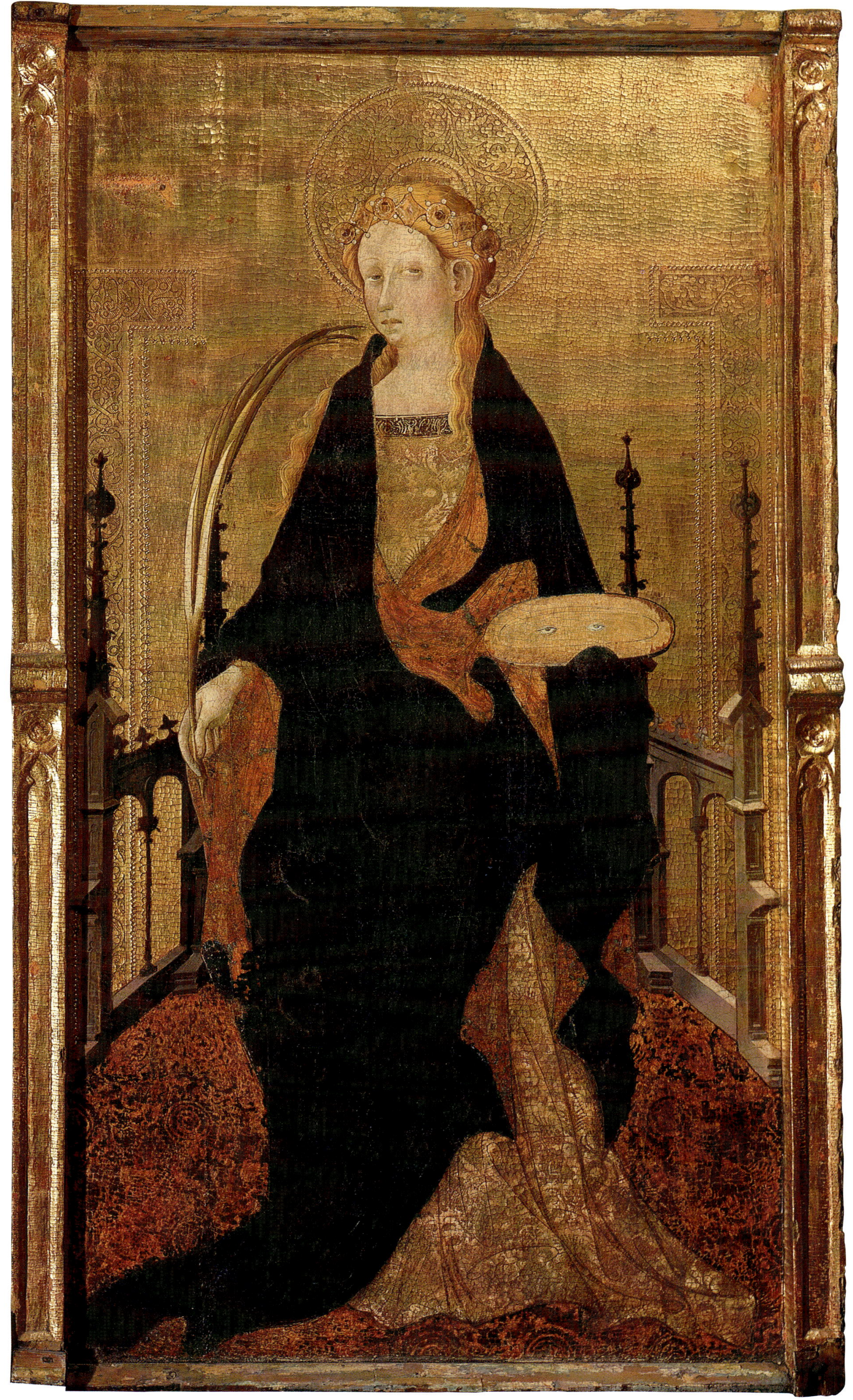

Figure 5-1

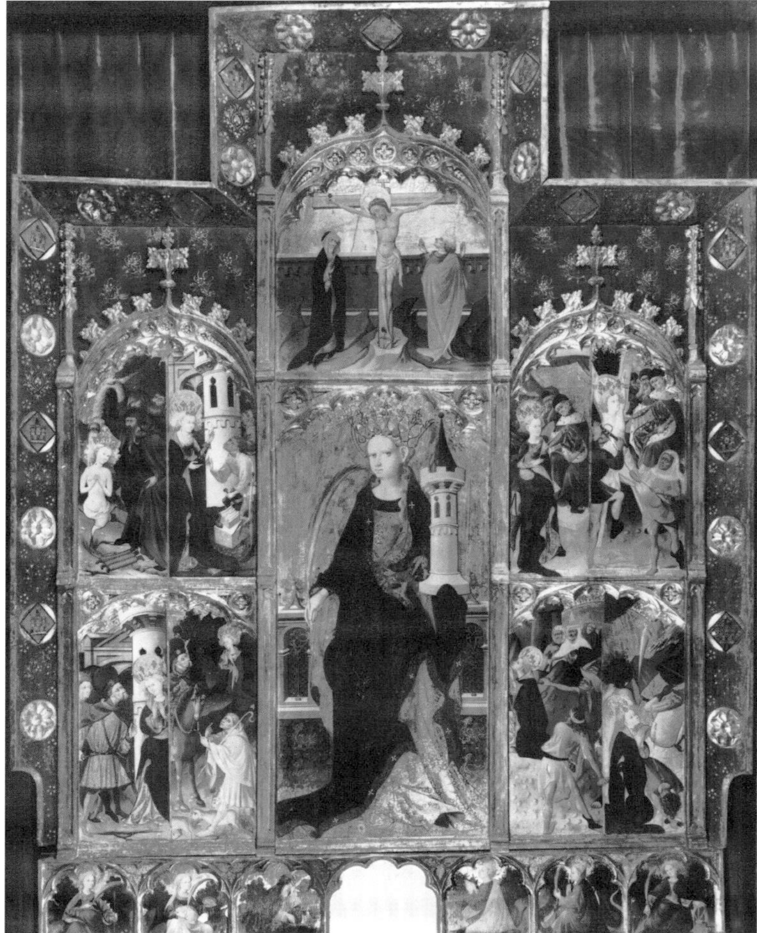

Figure 5-2

Gonçal Peris de Sarrià's workshop produced a large number of altarpieces, some of them known by document, others grouped stylistically around a documented work, the *Heads of Kings of Aragon,* painted in collaboration with Jaume Mateu and Joan Moreno for the *Casa de la Ciutat* of Valencia in 1427.[4] Some controversy remains about the length and scope of this painter's career, for three sets of documents exist that, until recently, were thought to refer to the same person (sometimes called simply Gonçal Peris, other times called Gonçal Peris de Sarrià, and still other times, Gonçal Sarrià). These documents are now believed to refer to an uncle and a nephew, but making the distinction is complicated by the fact that around Valencia, the surname Peris or Perez is as common as Smith is in New England.[5] What is known is that Peris de Sarrià's shop not only produced a sizeable number of altarpieces for Valencia, but that they also fashioned them for churches and monasteries beyond the Crown of Aragon. Several were painted for the Aragonese area around Teruel, at least one for Castile (Burgo de Osma), and at least one—the *Retablo of St. Lucy*—for Andalusia. Considering that Andalusia and Castile were part of a foreign country in this period, we can safely say that Gonçal Peris de Sarrià's shop made works for the international market, and the *St. Lucy* is one example of this production.

1. Clark Museum, Williamstown, Mass., bill from Celestino Dupont, antiquarian of Seville, to Mr. Clark, dated December 29, 1924, stating: "Un tableau primitif provanant du convente de Ste. Claire de Ubeda de XVIe."

2. Verbal statement from Lluís Plandiura, who gave the panel to the museum. See Chandler R. Post, *A History of Spanish Painting,* III, Cambridge, Mass., 1930, 316.

3. H. Travers Newton, "The Restoration of the St. Lucy Panel," in H. Travers Newton and Judith Berg Sobré, "*Saint Lucy* Attributed to Gonçal Peris and Workshop Practices in the Early Fifteenth Century Crown of Aragon," in *Homenatge a Joan Ainaud de Lasarte,* Barcelona, 1995 (forthcoming).

4. See Joan Aliaga Morell, doctoral thesis entitled *Anàlisi dels documents i obres atribuïdes als pintors Gonçal Peris i Gonçal Sarrià,* Universitat Politècnica de València, Departament d' Historia del Art, 1994, 89.

5. For the latest study that separates these personalities, see Aliaga Morell, 1994, 17–25, 31–37.

Catalogue No. 6

CIRCLE OF RODRIGO AND FRANCESC DE OSONA

Active in Valencia, 1463–1518

Agony in the Garden, ca. 1490
Oil on panel
7 9/16 x 6 3/16 in.
Museum of Art, Rhode Island School of Design
Mary B. Jackson Fund
57.282

Christ kneels on a small rise in front of a rock formation in the middle ground, gazing upward at a small angel. In the foreground, the apostles James, John the Evangelist, and Peter sleep. The other apostles slumber in a group behind Christ at left, while a band of Roman soldiers appears at the right, led by Judas. In the background is a tiny subsidiary scene of Christ on the road to Calvary, which winds from a miniature Jerusalem, here depicted as a seaside city.

The function of this diminutive painting is unclear. Far too small to be part of a *retablo,* it was probably intended for private devotion, whether combined with other scenes in a tiny triptych or standing alone. Though there are examples of other such small altarpieces in Spanish painting, not enough of them survive in a consistent form to be able to draw any further conclusions, and no real attempt has been made to study them.

This painting has been attributed to Rodrigo de Osona the Younger (now known to be named Francesc) by Chandler Post.[1] Rodrigo de Osona and his son Francesc ran one of the most important painting workshops in Valencia during the last quarter of the fifteenth century and the first two decades of the sixteenth century, producing numerous *retablos* and other sacred panels.[2] Rodrigo was the dominant figure in this shop, for surviving documents mention Francesc only jointly with his father, though he did sign one work, an *Epiphany* in the Victoria and Albert Museum, London, as the son of Master Rodrigo (fig. 6-2). Both Osonas were adept at the technique of oil glazing on panel, which originated in northern Europe, and they were certainly conversant with Netherlandish compositional prototypes, probably from consulting imported prints and paintings.[3] They also were certainly in contact with Italian painters, at least two of whom, Paolo da San Leocadio and Francesco Pagano, were working in Valencia between 1472 and 1476.[4]

Late-fifteenth-century Valencia was the most cosmopolitan city on the Iberian Peninsula; it had superseded Barcelona as the Crown of Aragon's principal gateway to Mediterranean trade, and it enjoyed strong political connections with Italy. In addition, Valencia had a thriving commercial relationship with Flanders, including the importation of paintings by local merchants. It also had a resident Italian merchant colony.[5]

This cosmopolitanism is reflected in Valencian painting of the period and can certainly be seen in the *Agony in the Garden,* where both Netherlandish-style oil glazes (in the richly colored garments and shining armor) and a certain Italian-style breadth of spatial layout (though not perfect perspective) can be seen. But characteristics peculiar to Valencia are also present, most particularly in the landscape, which differs from its northern counterparts in its intense sense of light, appropriate to a more southern latitude, and in its foliage. Landscape settings are found in paintings from many Valencian workshops during the last half of the fifteenth century, but far less frequently elsewhere on the Iberian Peninsula. Marinescapes are found nowhere else.

The general style of the figures—the haloes with rays within them and the landscape with its tiny marinescape (replete with ships) to each side of the city of Jerusalem—do have affinities with works by Rodrigo and Francesc de Osona, but the facial types are somewhat different and suggest either a follower or an independent master, though certainly one within the Osona stylistic orbit.[6] However, it is also possible that the extremely small size of this painting—no larger than a manuscript illumination—may have affected the style of painting, especially if the painter was accustomed to the large scale of *retablo* painting. An extensive tradition of manuscript illumination existed in Valencia during the fourteenth and fifteenth centuries; however, this painting's fine oil glaze technique on wood suggests a panel painter rather than an illuminator, who would have had a somewhat different technique.[7]

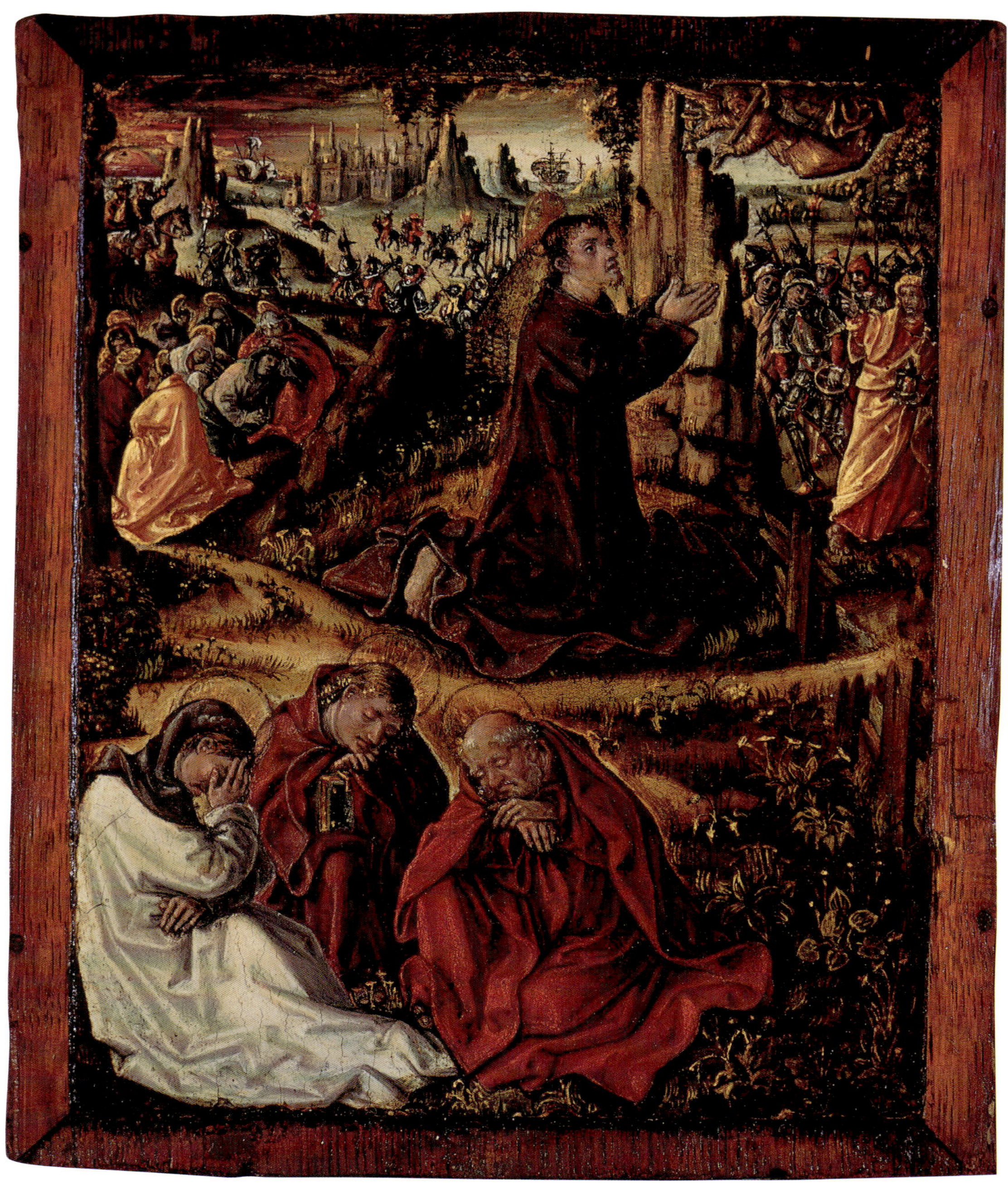

Figure 6-1

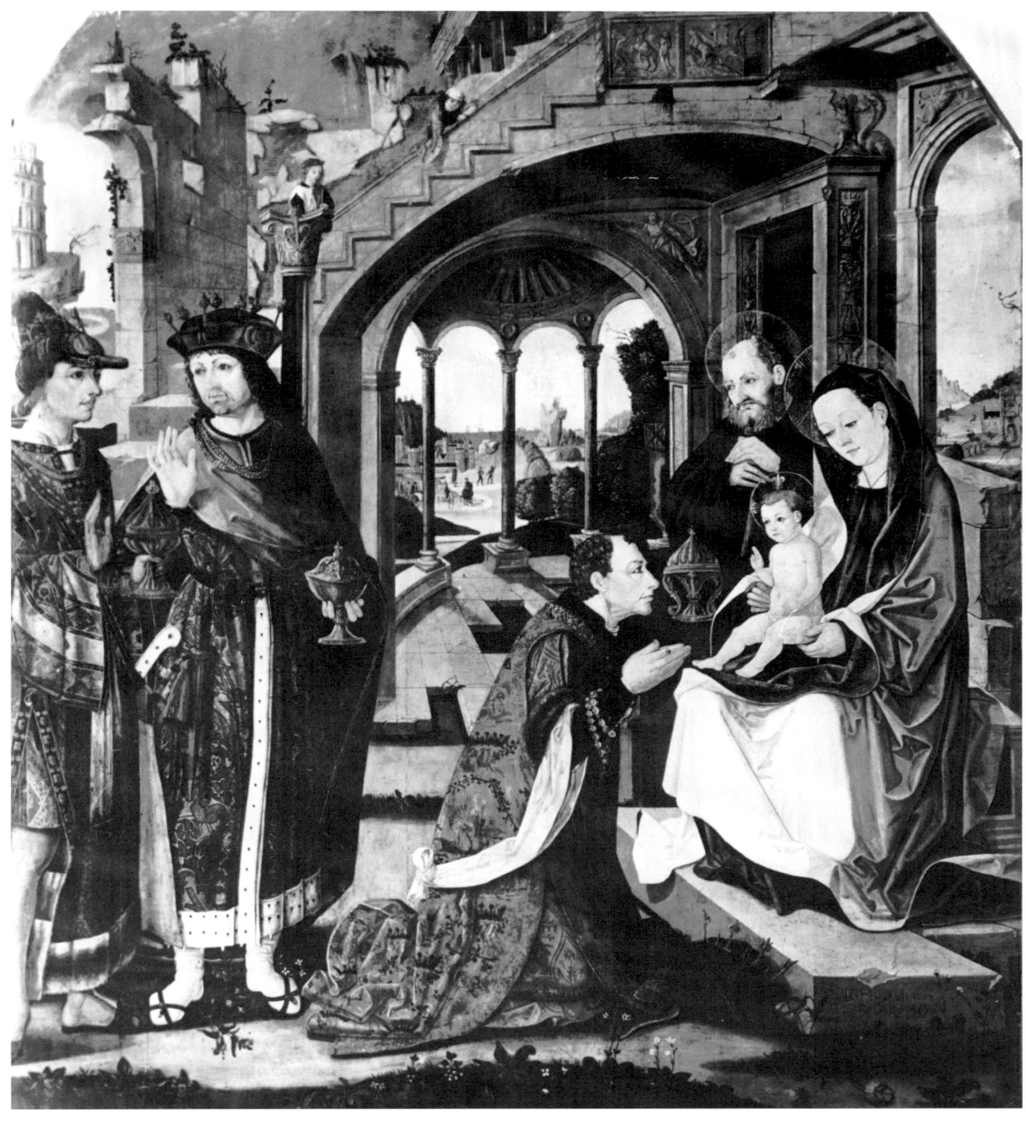

Figure 6-2

The theme of the *Agony in the Garden* was particularly popular in Valencia during the fifteenth century; it is found, for example, in other works by the Osonas, in a panel by a Valencian follower of Bermejo, and in at least five versions from the studio of Paolo da San Leocadio.[8] All of them contain the same iconographic elements: the three sleeping apostles in the foreground, Christ and the angel (the latter always smaller in hierarchical scale), and the Roman soldiers walking up from Jerusalem led by Judas. The composition to which this tiny *Agony* is closest is a large panel by Paolo da San Leocadio, in the collection of the marqués de Montortal (fig. 6-3), probably executed in Gandía. The latter also has the subsidiary group of eight sleeping apostles, although it lacks the *Via Dolorosa* episode. This composition and Paolo's other variations on it have been traced to German prints, notably those of Martin Schongauer and Master I. A. M. De Zwolle.[9] The style of the little *Agony*, however, appears to be earlier, squarely within the context of the late fifteenth century, which suggests that this particular composition—and perhaps the same German prints as sources—was simply part of the Valencian stylistic and iconographic vocabulary at this time. The transformation of Jerusalem to a coastal city seems to be the fantasy of this painter alone.

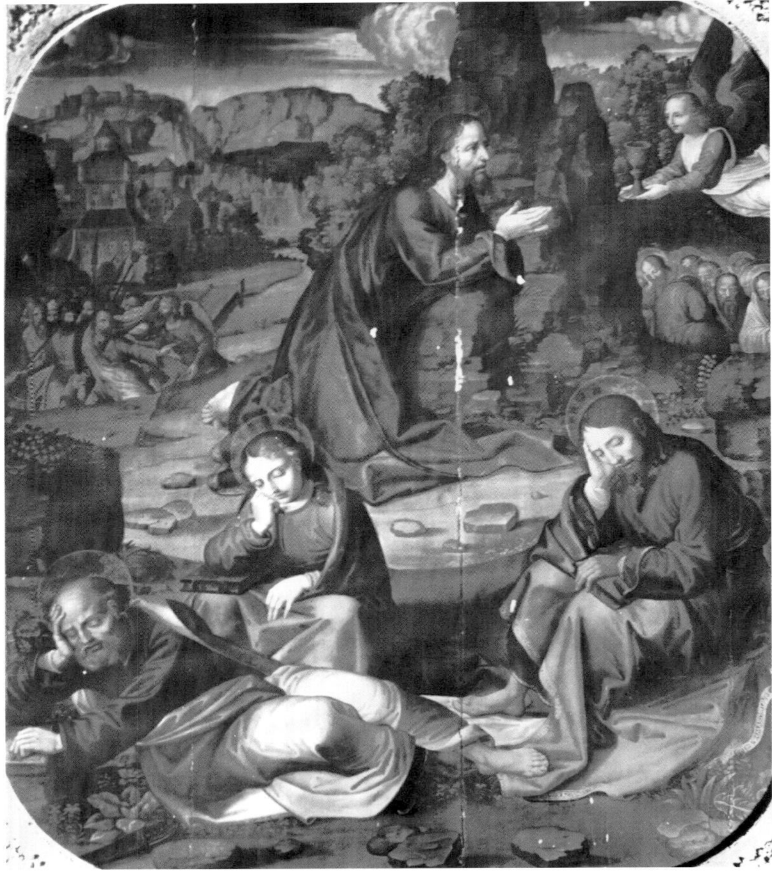

Figure 6-3

1. Chandler R. Post, "An Agony in the Garden by Rodrigo de Osona, the Younger," *Bulletin of the Rhode Island School of Design* 45 (1958), 1–3. The attribution was reiterated by Post in *A History of Spanish Painting,* XIII, Cambridge, Mass., 1966, 342. Until the discovery of a document naming Rodrigo de Osona's son as Francesc, scholars designated him as Rodrigo II or Rodrigo de Osona the Younger. For these documents, see Ximo Company i Climent and Luisa Tolosa, "La identidad del pintor Osona el Joven," *Archivo Español de Arte* 252 (1990), 666–667.

2. For the best recent studies of the Osonas, see Ximo Company i Climent, *La Pintura dels Osona, una crülla d'hispanismes, flamenquismes i italianismes,* 2 vols., Lleida, Pagés editors, 1991.

3. Ximo Company i Climent (*El Mundo de los Osonas,* Valencia, Museu Sant Pius II, 1994, 49–66) postulates an actual trip to Flanders by Rodrigo, perhaps between 1465 and 1470, when he was undocumented in Valencia.

4. Paolo da San Leocadio settled in Valencia and subsequently practiced his craft in Gandía. See Ximo Company i Climent, *Pintura del Renaixement al Ducat de Gandía,* Valencia, Institució Alfons el Magnànim, 1985, 33–38, for a study of the career of Paolo da San Leocadio.

5. See, for example, Gianni Rebora, "I primi patroni dell Annunziata: I Della Chiesa una grande famiglia di mercanti internazionali," in *Bartolomé Bermejo e Il Trittico di Acqui,* Acqui Terme, L' Ancora, 1988, 17–31.

6. Ximo Company i Climent, 1991, I, 103, believes it to be a follower's work.

7. Valencia had an active manuscript-illuminating industry dating from the fourteenth century, but except for the unusual case of the fourteenth-century court artist Ferrer Bassa, no record of manuscript illuminators in Valencia who also executed panel paintings exists. See Amparo Villalba Davalos, *La miniatura valenciana en los siglos XIV y XV,* Valencia, Institución Alfonso el Magnánimo, 1964, 259–273, for a list of documented manuscript painters from about 1468 to 1500; she also has a chapter on Valencian manuscript painters in the second half of the fifteenth century (153–204).

8. See Ximo Company i Climent, 1994, 164.

9. Ximo Company i Climent, 1991, 166–167. For another example, see a similar version in a private collection also believed to have come from Gandía and dated ca. 1507, illustrated in ibid., 165.

Catalogue No. 7

ANONYMOUS MUDÉJAR CRAFTSMAN
Active in Manises (near Valencia)

Bowl with the Arms of Aragon and Sicily, ca. 1465
Metallic glazed ceramic
18 7/8 in. diameter
The Minneapolis Institute of Arts
The Christina N. and Swan J. Turnblad Memorial Fund, 1962
62.11

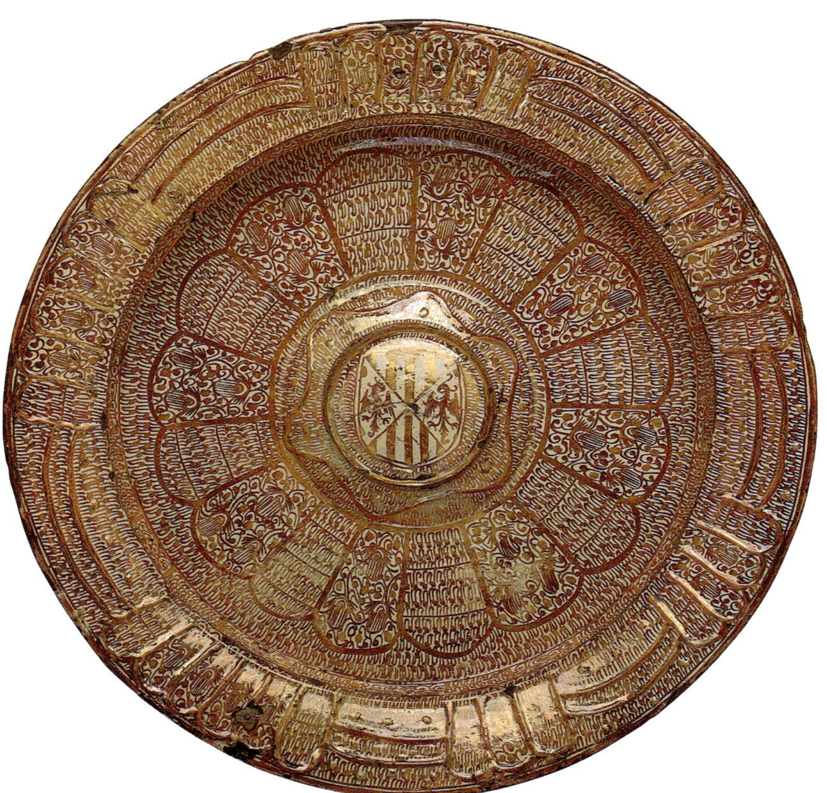

Figure 7

This deep, round bowl is decorated with curvilinear and geometric designs in gold-colored metallic glaze. The arms of Aragon and Sicily occupy a medallion in its center. The dating of this piece hinges on the coat of arms. Sicily had been united to the Crown of Aragon since 1282, at first mainly by rule of a younger branch of the Aragonese royal house. But from the time of Martin I, it was ruled directly by the main branch, first under the indigenous Aragonese line descending from the counts of Barcelona, and later, with the accession of Fernando I de Antequera, under the Trastámaras.

The bowl comes from the pottery workshops of Manises, near Valencia. Along with nearby Paterna, Manises was virtually a one-industry town. The majority of its inhabitants and its chief ceramists were Mudéjars, Muslims resident in the Christian kingdoms of Spain who had originally brought their craft, and particularly their technique of metallic glazing, from Muslim Al-Andalus several centuries earlier. Early on, Islamic techniques and decorative motifs and French and Italian decorative elements had fused to create a distinctive style, which continued to evolve over the years. By 1350, the industry was thriving, and it became one of the Valencian region's chief export products.[1]

Part of the reason for the growth of this industry was its technique of mass production: once the kilns were built, they could be used not only to fire tiles and pottery, but also modest products such as ceramic sugar molds.[2] Quality depended on individual craftsmen; some specialized in crude ware, while others, very highly skilled, made fine vessels on commission. The reputation of Manises ware was such that by the mid fourteenth century, its ceramists were sent abroad, not only to install the tile floors their workshops made, but sometimes to build kilns and to fashion the tiles on the spot.[3] Bills of lading from the fourteenth and fifteenth centuries speak of shipments of ceramics to Florence, Ferrara, Siena, England, Bruges, and Venice—the last, through her extensive shipping empire, reciprocally supplying the raw materials of lead and tin for the glazes. The extent of the trade can be seen pictorially: a Manises blue-and-gold *bote* ("jar") figures prominently in the foreground of the center panel of Hugo van der Goes' *Portinari Altarpiece.*

The real glamour trade in these ceramics came in custom orders of high quality pieces for European nobility. Examples survive of bowls, plates, and other vessels with coats of arms, including those of the royal house of Portugal, the dukes of Burgundy, the Republic of Florence, and the queen of Aragon, María of Castile, to give only a few examples.[4]

The *Bowl with the Arms of Aragon and Sicily* belongs in this group of commissioned fine ceramics. The complex decorative designs have similarities to plate made for the Catholic King Fernando, now in the Instituto de Valencia de Don Juan in Madrid, which bears the arms of Naples.[5] It has been dated to the early years of the sixteenth century, both for political reasons and because of some Italian Renaissance decorative motifs that are incorporated into its ornamentation.[6] It is harder to date the *Bowl with the Arms of Aragon and Sicily* since the coat of arms is found throughout the fifteenth century. A case could be made that it would predate the union of Castile and Aragon under the Catholic Kings, or before 1474, since from that time the coats of arms of Castile/León and Aragon/Sicily are usually joined, as can be seen in the *Royal Arms of the Catholic Kings* (fig. 12). The decorative motifs in the bowl, with their tightly woven clusters and the total filling of the surface, lack any Renaissance references. Even though the Mudéjars of Manises had by this time lived for centuries under Christian rule, the persistent custom of filling all available surfaces with design points back to the bowl's Islamic roots and is an excellent example of the fusion of two cultures, Muslim and Christian, into an object that is, in the final analysis, characteristically Hispanic.

1. A. González Martí, *Cerámica del Levante español,* I, Madrid-Barcelona, Editorial Laber, 1944, 4.

2. J. G. Osma, *Los maestros alfareros de Manises, Paterna y Valencia* (2nd Ed.), Madrid, 1923, 12.

3. Three of these workers were at work at Avignon for Cardinal Aubert Audon between 1358 and 1362, while another, Jehan de Valencia, set up a studio and directed it at Poitiers from 1384 to 1386. See Osma, 1923, 30 ff.

4. González Martí, 1944, 26.

5. Illustrated in *Reyes y Mecenas, Los Reyes Católicos, Maximiliano I y los inicios de la Casa de Austria en España*, Madrid, Electa, 1992, 427, fig. 164.

6. B. Martínez Caviro, *La loza dorada*, Madrid, Editora Nacional, 1983, 173.

Catalogue No. 8

ANONYMOUS ANDALUSIAN MASTER
Active in Andalusia

Virgin and Child with Female Saint and St. Jerome, ca. 1465
Tempera, oil, and gold leaf on panel
20 3/8 x 13 3/4 in.
The Metropolitan Museum of Art
The Friedsam Collection
Bequest of Michael Friedsam, 1931
32.100.105

The Virgin sits on a throne adorned with columns, a parapeted canopy, a white brocaded drape, and two niches with the small figures of the Virgin Annunciate and the Angel Gabriel. The nude Christ Child reclines on Mary's lap, resting on a white cloth. He holds a flower of undetermined species. To the right is St. Jerome, while a female saint holds the end of Christ's cloth at left. The floor is tiled. The wall has a brocaded panel for two-thirds of its height. The portion above it is black.[1] The painting is small in size and evidently intended for private devotion.[2]

There are some unsettled iconographical questions about this panel. The female saint has been identified in one instance as St. Catherine of Alexandria.[3] Though she holds none of Catherine's traditional attributes (sword, wheel, martyr's palm), the rich brocaded robe she wears and her crown may be references to that saint's aristocratic station. Her solicitous gesture toward the Christ Child may perhaps be a reference to Catherine's vision of a mystical marriage with him. St. Jerome is accompanied by his lion (his most famous symbol, but one that is actually appropriated from the legend of a different hermit saint). He is not dressed in the traditional cardinal's robe, which would be an allusion to his role as papal secretary, but rather in the gray robe of the Hieronymite order. The Virgin wears her traditional (now darkened) blue mantle, but she is also clearly in the role of Queen of Heaven, for her dress beneath the cloak is rich brocade, and she, like the female saint, wears a crown. The saints have haloes of rays. Christ's halo is of cruciform rays, while the Virgin's has not only bigger rays, but also a sturdy gold-leaf disk backing it up.

The large brocade pattern in the background and the delicate white brocade behind the Virgin's throne are the chief clues to a regional identity for this panel, for they are typical of Andalusian painting during the third quarter of the fifteenth century, which tends to combine many large patterns within a single panel while contrasting them with delicate detail. These traits are found not only in small panels such as this one, but also in much larger ones. As in contemporaneous Castilian painting, there are references—though here quite distant—to Netherlandish painting. This resemblance is seen most noticeably in the Christ Child, whose reclining posture (though flipped) dimly evokes the tiny *Madonna at the Fireplace* by Robert Campin in the Hermitage in St. Petersburg. The medium used in this Andalusian work, however, is not a Netherlandish oil glaze. Rather, it is a mixture of tempera and oil, a common combination throughout fourteenth-century and fifteenth-century Spain. Though the meticulous application of oil glazes popularized in Flanders during the early fifteenth century did eventually come to be practiced over most of the Iberian Peninsula as the fifteenth century wore on, oil had been used in combination with tempera far longer; indeed, most medieval painters used a mixture of different media in the same panel, depending on what pigments they used. These media could include egg yolk, walnut oil, linseed oil, gum, and glue.

Attempts have been made to attribute this little painting to two different Andalusian workshops, those of Juan Sánchez de Castro and Juan Nuñez, but neither attribution seems convincing.[4] It is difficult to attempt an attribution of this little painting to any known Andalusian studio or master; indeed, it is difficult to draw many conclusions about fifteenth-century Andalusian painting at all, because very little of it survives. Other parts of Spain have lost medieval works to wars and other political upheavals, but Andalusian, particularly late medieval Sevillian painting, was intentionally discarded in the sixteenth and seventeenth centuries. At that time, the great prosperity of the area due to New World trade prompted churches and donors to replace most of their old *retablos* with new ones. These better conformed to the new iconographical dictates inspired by the Council of

Trent.[5] Even paintings that were not part of *retablos* did not escape unscathed, but for other reasons. Many of the great icons of the Virgin found in Sevillian churches, for instance, have been so venerated as miraculous images that continual repainting and embellishment have all but obscured the originals.[6]

While no painter's name can reliably be connected with the *Virgin and Child with Female Saint and St. Jerome,* some features do further link it with Andalusia, and particularly with Seville. The composition shows similarities to one by Juan Sánchez de Castro, the fragmentary *Virgin of the Rosary,* originally from the church of San Julián in Seville and now in the Cathedral, which depicts the enthroned Virgin and Child between St. Peter and Jerome.[7] It has also been suggested that the Hieronymite habit of St. Jerome might connect the owner of this small painting to the monastery of San Isidoro del Campo, which, though originally Cistercian, was taken over by the Hieronymite order in 1431.[8] Finally, there is the lyrical charm of the painting, a charm that has traditionally been said to characterize Andalusian art from this period—and for centuries to come.

1. Chandler Post (*A History of Spanish Painting,* VI, Cambridge, Mass., 1935, 650) believes that the black was once blue, but is now darkened.

2. Post, ibid., calls the panel the center of a triptych, but no evidence of a set of wings exists.

3. Museum records, The Metropolitan Museum of Art.

4. August L. Meyer ("Miscelánea," *Revista española de arte* 2 [1933], 304–305) makes the attribution to Juan Sánchez de Castro, while Post suggests Juan Nuñez.

5. See Jesús M. Palomero Páramo, *El retablo sevillano del renacimiento, analísis y evolución,* Seville, Excma. Diputación Provincial de Sevilla, 1983, 15.

6. José Gudiol Ricart, *Ars Hispaniae: Pintura Gótica,* Madrid, Editorial Plus Ultra, 1955, 192.

7. Illustrated in Gudiol Ricart, 1955, 391, fig. 335.

8. See Alfredo J. Moreles, María Jesús Sanz, Juan Miguel Serrera, and Enrique Valdivieso, *Guía Artística de Seville y su Provincia,* Seville, Excma. Diputación Provincial de Sevilla, n.d. (1984?), 545. Post, 1935, 650, made the initial suggestion about the Hieronymites.

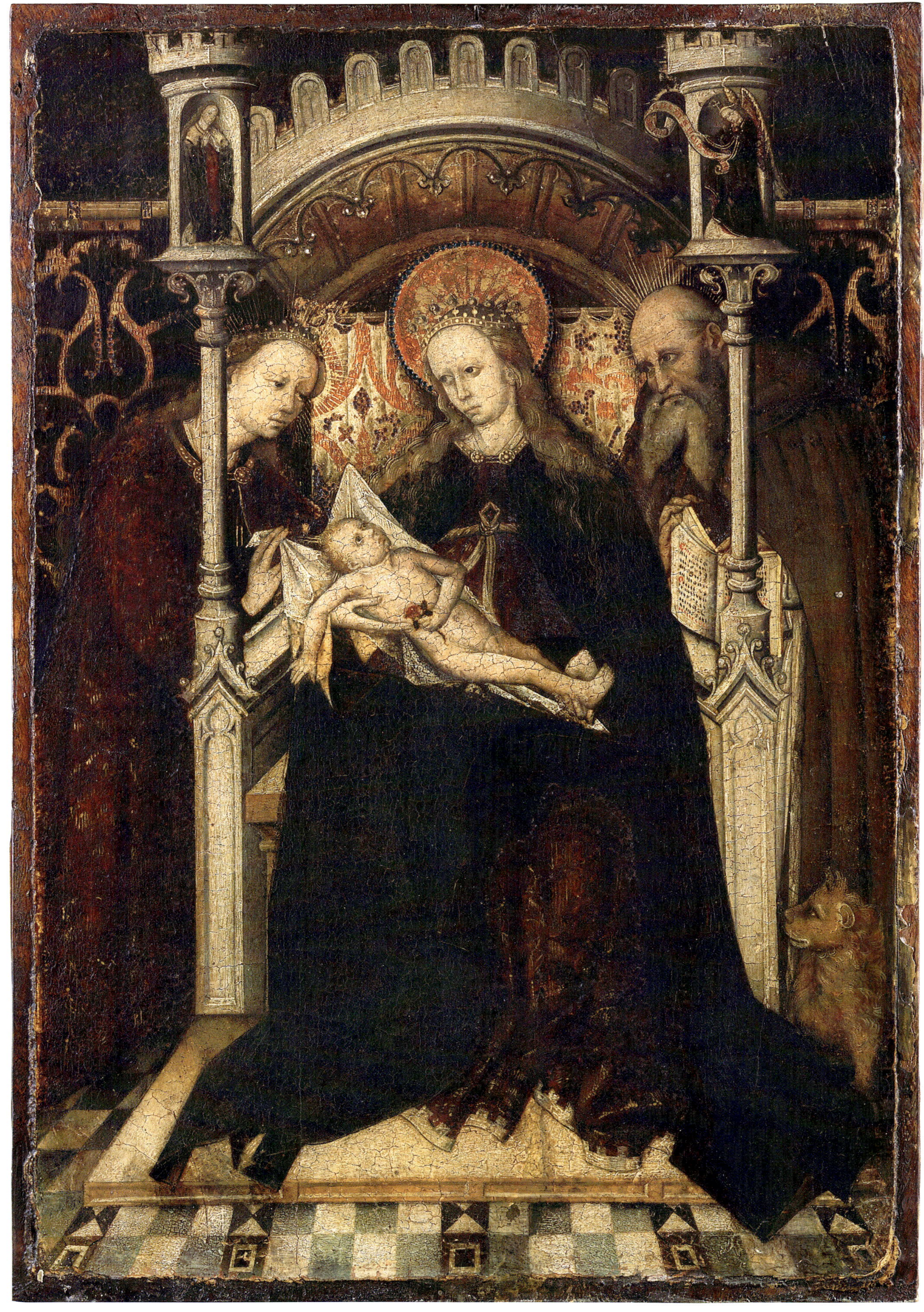

Figure 8

Catalogue No. 9

MASTER OF THE CATHOLIC KINGS

Active in Castile, ca. 1495–1500

The Presentation in the Temple
Oil on panel
62 x 38 in.
Fogg Art Museum
Harvard University Art Museums
Francis H. Burr Fund and Anonymous Gifts
1933.29

The Virgin presents the Christ Child to the High Priest Simeon in the temple. She holds the Child out to him over an altar covered by a white cloth. Mary is dressed in her traditional blue mantle and white wimple, while Simeon, bald but bearded, wears a brocaded robe with a purple, ermine-lined hood over a fur-trimmed red robe. Around this group are eight other figures—six male, two female—the most prominent being the lady who carries a basket with two doves at the left; she wears a red dress with a brocaded underskirt. The temple is here envisioned as a Gothic church, which has a screen embellished with the sculpted figures of two prophets separating the nave from the apse. On the walls of the screen are coats of arms; additional coats of arms appear in the pendentives of the crossing, in one of the crossing windows, in the windows of the apse, and on the aisle wall at left. One of the nave clerestory windows has the stained-glass image of a saint. A canopy with an inscription hangs over the altar.

This panel is one of eight surviving panels belonging to a large *retablo*, whose panels are now dispersed among several museums and a private collection. The other panels are the *Annunciation* and *Nativity* (San Francisco Museum of Fine Arts), the *Visitation* (University of Arizona Museum of Art, Tucson), *Adoration of the Magi* (Denver Art Museum), *Circumcision* (private collection, England), *Marriage at Cana*, and *Christ Among the Doctors* (both National Gallery of Art, Washington, D.C.).[1] The altarpiece is believed to have been commissioned by the Catholic Kings Fernando and Isabel on the occasion of the marriage of their children, Juan and Juana, to Margaret and Philip, the children of Maximilian I, Holy Roman Emperor, in 1496/7. The reason for this inference is the profusion of heraldry in the *Presentation in the Temple* and in several other panels in the series, which include the arms of the Catholic Kings (containing the heraldic elements seen in the *Royal Arms of the Catholic Kings,* fig. 12), the Hapsburg double-headed eagle, the arms of Burgundy, and monograms of Maximilian and of Fernando and Isabel.[2]

It has long been suggested that this *retablo* came from a church in Valladolid, but no evidence exists to substantiate this claim.[3] The size of the panels does suggest that they were originally part of a large high altar *retablo*, similar to many others in Castile, which were dedicated partly or wholly to Christ and/or the Virgin. The large panels would have been arranged in two or more horizontal tiers flanking a taller central vertical strip containing painted or sculpted images, arranged above a *banco* with images of Old Testament prophets or saints. The arrangement would be much like the slightly later *retablo mayor* of the Avila Cathedral (fig. 9-2) and like it, this altarpiece would have curved to conform to the shape of the apse.

Several scholars have remarked upon and studied the profusion of Netherlandish compositional references in the panels, which suggest a master or masters familiar with a variety of northern sources.[4] The closest resemblance in the *Presentation in the Temple* is found in the pose of the lady with the basket of doves, which echoes the pose of the lady at left in Rogier van der Weyden's *Columba Altarpiece*—though the Hispanic painters have changed the color of her dress from green to red. The high priest and the Virgin are also similarly positioned, though the Christ Child is reversed. The setting, though, is substantially different: the master of this panel paints a flat-apsed church interior, van der Weyden a rounded-apsed temple. Other references to Netherlandish painting include the treatment of lighting (with the nave of the temple in shadow but the apse area lit), the fine painting of garment textures, and the nature of the drapery folds.

Art historians have long called Spanish painting and sculpture during the last half of the fifteenth century "Hispano-Flemish," as if Spain were an artistic fiefdom of the Netherlands. In the the Crown of Aragon (with a few

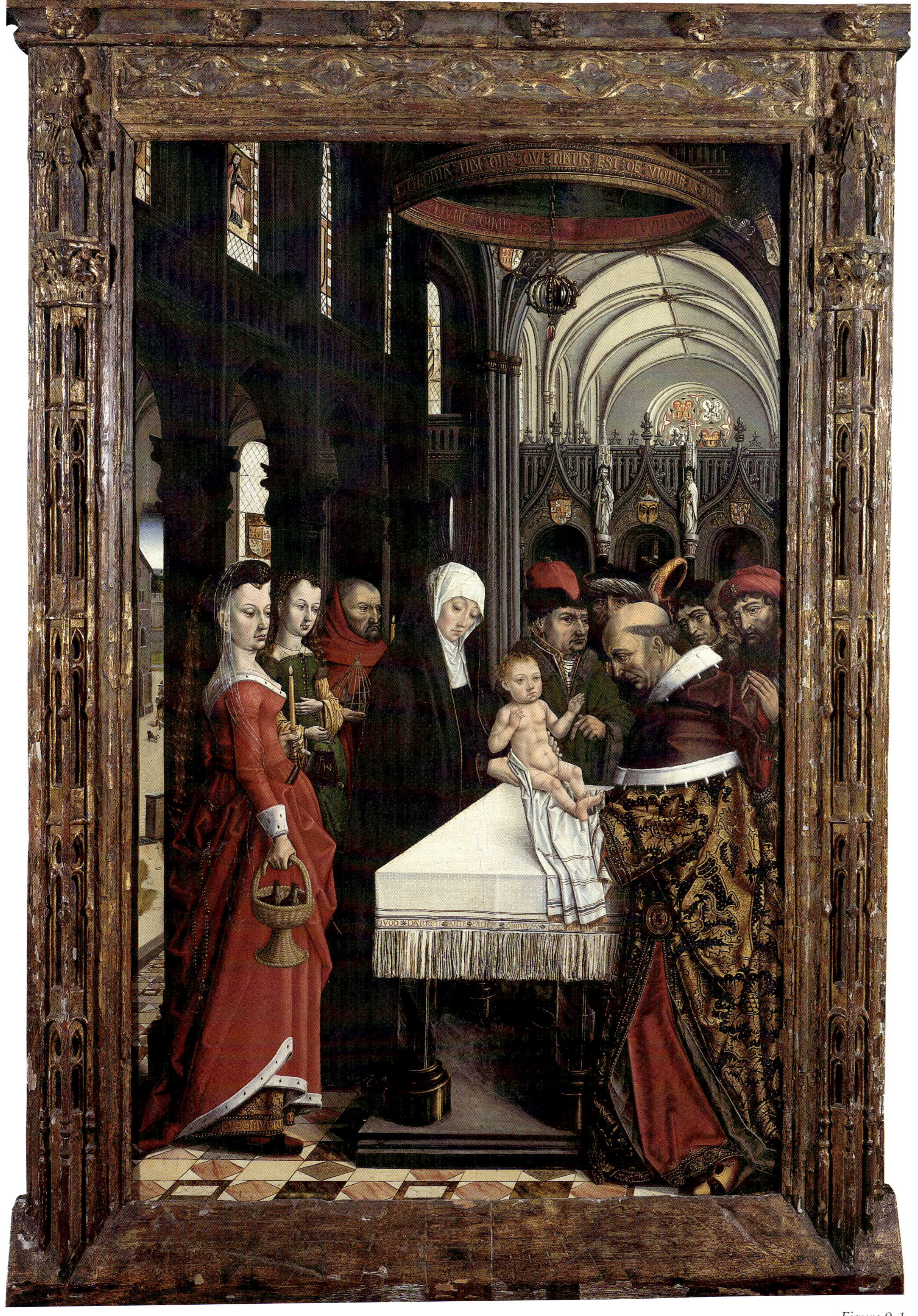

Figure 9-1

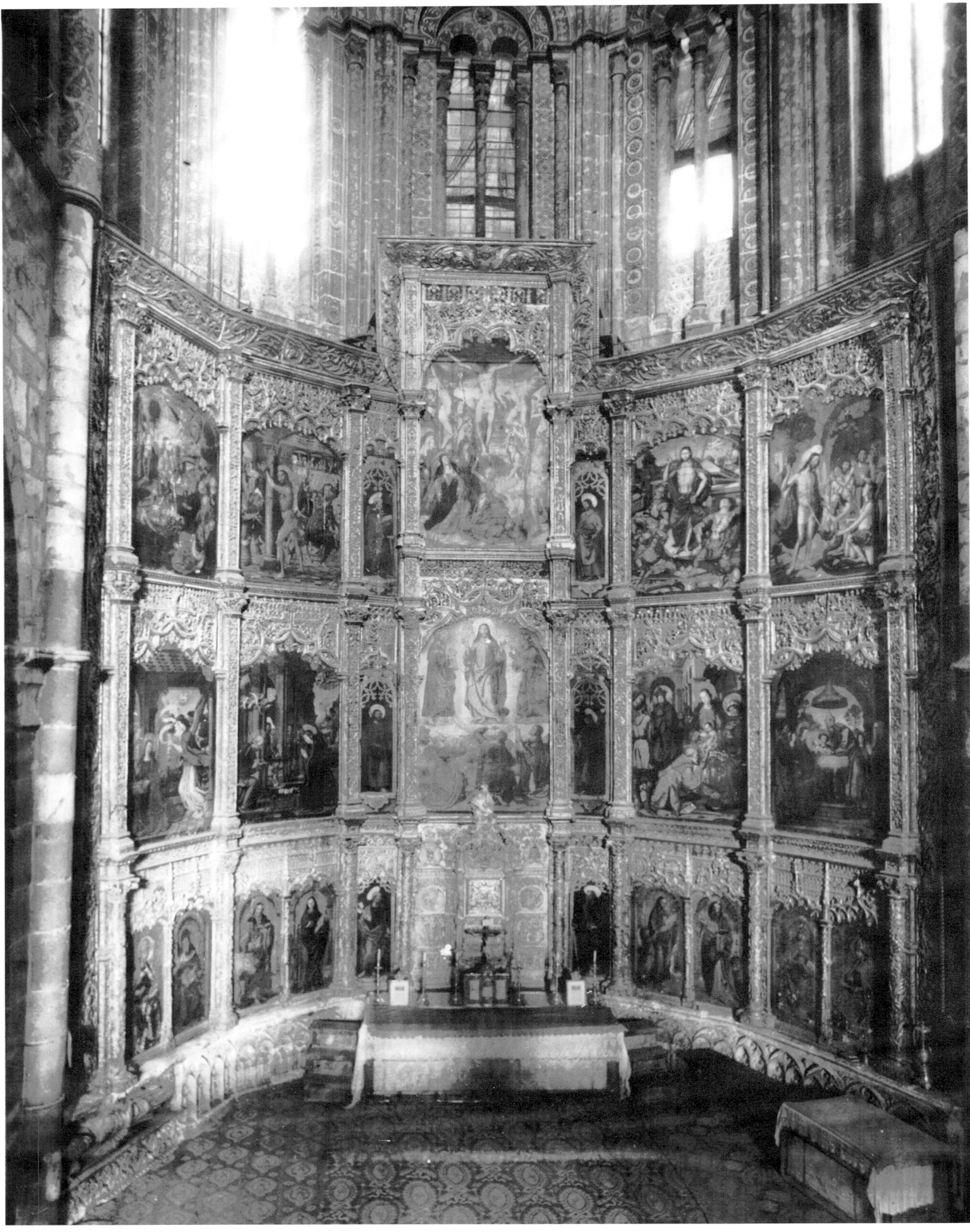

Figure 9-2

exceptions, such as Lluís Dalmau, Rodrigo de Osona, and Bermejo), there was actually little stylistic affinity between Northern European and local painting, aside from the widespread use of German and Flemish prints for compositional sources—a logical practice in a period when compositions were borrowed with impunity.[5] Castile had closer commercial ties with Flanders, England, and northern France, and its nobility had more cosmopolitan tastes, but even here, the Netherlandish influence was variable. To be sure, some northern painters were working on the peninsula, among them Jorge Inglés, the still-unidentified Master of Sopetran, and Isabel's court painters, Juan de Flandes and Michel Sittow. Other painters, such as Pedro Berruguete, may have had some training abroad with a Netherlandish painter (in Berruguete's case in somewhat unusual circumstances for he trained with Josse van Wassenhove of Ghent at the Italian court of Urbino). Still others may have learned some of their craft in the workshop of one of the northerners working on the Iberian Peninsula. But other Castilian painters, like their Aragonese counterparts and painters elsewhere in Europe, picked up their Flemish traits solely by appropriating compositions and style conventions from northern paintings or prints.[6]

In the case of the Master of the Catholic Kings workshop, however, both the compositional and the stylistic derivations bespeak painters who had a more intimate knowledge of northern sources than most of their Castilian contemporaries. Some earlier scholars suggested that these panels were painted by a still-unidentified Flemish master resident in Spain, while other scholars sought to attribute the panels to the workshop of the Castilian painter Diego de la Cruz, active in Castile between 1488 and 1499; both theories have since been discounted.[7] Indeed, to this point, no one has been able to establish a convincing relationship between the painters of these panels and any other painter on the Iberian Peninsula. On the other hand, the facial traits and the warm-toned color scheme of these paintings suggest indigenous artists, and technical analysis has shown that the panels were definitely painted in Castile, using specifically Castilian techniques to prepare the panels for painting.[8]

It is also apparent that more than one painter worked on the Catholic Kings *retablo.* Three different styles have been isolated, one group being responsible for the *Annunciation, Nativity, Visitation,* and *Adoration of the Magi,* a second for the *Presentation in the Temple,* the *Marriage at Cana,* and *Christ among the Doctors,* and a third for the *Circumcision.*[9] It was not unusual for several painters to work on large Castilian *retablos.* In the immense *retablo mayor* of Santa María del Castillo, for example, there were three painters at work, and they may have done their work in separate shops—for even the haloes differ between some of the panels—only assembling them upon installation.[10] The *retablo* of the Catholic Kings was probably all done in one workshop since all of the paintings (with the possible exception of *Christ among the Doctors)* have similar settings, drapery types, and heraldry. It appears more likely that the workshop, presumably organized under one master, portioned out panels among distinct groups of workers, so that while stylistic details may differ, the overall look is the same, and the altarpiece, once installed, would have appeared unified.

The unusual reliance on so many northern sources within one altarpiece and the conscious attempt to emulate a Flemish style suggest that this group of Castilian painters was striving to rise to the taste and standards of its royal patrons. The Catholic Kings, and Isabel in particular, demonstrated a marked preference for things authentically Netherlandish, and perhaps they commissioned this particular master and his shop because their painting style was the best local substitute at that particular moment for the real thing. The master and his shop then produced an altarpiece that, for all its Castilian format, for once justifies the term Hispano-Flemish.

1. All the panels are reproduced in Richard Mann, *Spanish Paintings of the Fifteenth through Nineteenth Centuries,* National Gallery of Art, Washington, D.C., Cambridge University Press, 1990, 95–97, 103.

2. Colin Eisler, *Paintings from the Samuel H. Kress Collection: European Schools Excluding Italian,* Oxford, Phaidon Press, 1977, 178.

3. Theory postulated by A. Van der Put in an unpublished typescript, quoted by Richard Mann, 1990, 99, note 3, on the basis that the Catholic Kings favored the city of Valladolid, but no evidence corroborates this provenance.

4. Eisler, 1977, 178–182; Mann, 1990, 98; Chandler R. Post, *A History of Spanish Painting,* IV, Cambridge, Mass., Harvard University Press, 1933, 422–423; Charles Cuttler, *Northern Painting from Pucelle to Bruegel,* New York, Holt Rinehart and Winston, 1968, 254.

5. See Pilar Silva Maroto, "Influencia de los grabados nórdicos en la pintura hispanoflamenca," *Archivo Español de Arte* 61 (1988), 271–290, and Francisco Conti, "Juan de la Abadía el Viejo y Roger van der Weyden," *Archivo Español de Arte* 60 (1987), 463–468.

6. Pilar Silva Maroto, *Pintura hispanoflamenca castellana: Burgos y Palencia,* I, Madrid, Junta de Castilla y León, 1990, 40–57.

7. The northern source theory was proposed by J. V. L. Brans, *Isabel la Católica y el arte Hispano-Flamenco,* Madrid, 1952, 130–133. Diego de la Cruz was suggested by José Gudiol Ricart, "El pintor Diego de la Cruz," *Goya* 70 (1966), 208. The latter suggestion was disputed by Mann, 1990, 92, and also by Pilar Silva Maroto, 1990, II, 368.

8. Mann, 1990, 98. Mann's observations on the technical analyses of the panels (93 and 101) note the presence of fibers (which he quotes as grass) found in the initial layers of the gesso ground. These fibers are probably hemp, which is consistent with ground preparation in Castilian painting.

9. Gudiol Ricart, 1966, 214–215; Mann, 1990, 98.

10. Judith Berg Sobré, *Behind the Altar Table,* Columbia, Mo., University of Missouri Press, 1989, 25.

Catalogue No. 10

PEDRO BERRUGUETE
Active in Castile, 1477–1504

The Assumption of the Virgin
Oil and gold leaf on panel
56 x 36 in.
Davis Museum and Cultural Center
Wellesley College
1965.52

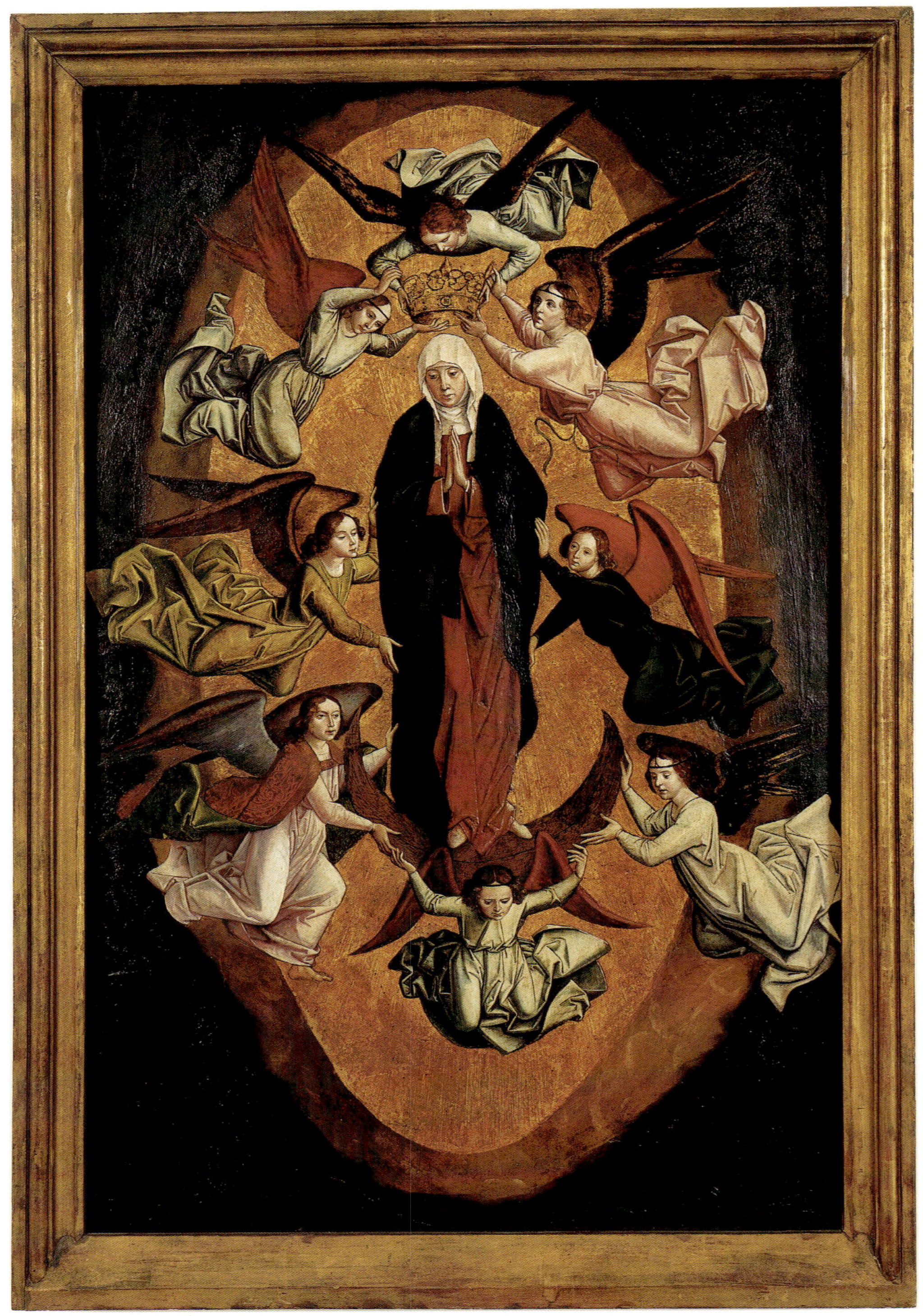

Figure 10-1

The Virgin Mary, standing on a crescent moon, is borne heavenward by five angels. Three hold the moon, while two nominally support her body at the sides. Three additional angels, two at either side and one at the top, complete the symmetry of the composition by holding a sumptuous crown above her head. The Virgin is dressed in her traditional red robe, blue mantle, and white wimple. The angels wear varicolored robes, mostly pastel, ranging from white to pink to light and dark blue to light olive. Their wings are of more intense hues, including red, bronze, and deep blue. The angel at the lower left also wears a brocaded cope. All the figures are arranged in front of a gilded *mandorla*, which fades out to a duller gold, and in turn is set against a deep blue sky.

This painting is characteristic of Pedro Berruguete's style. Berruguete, like Martín Bernat, came from the minor nobility. His family, of Basque origins, settled in Castile, at Tierra de Campos. He was born in Paredes de Nava, near Palencia, but the exact place and date of his training is uncertain.[1] Scholars commonly believe, however, that Berruguete can be identified with the Pietro Spagnuolo documented at the court of Federigo da Montefeltro in Urbino in 1477.[2] Affinities in his style to that of Josse van Wassenhove of Ghent, also at Urbino (in 1473), as well as a mastery of Italianate perspective and the presence of classical allusions in some of his architectural settings, seem to support this identification.

If Berruguete was indeed in Urbino, he did not linger there. By 1483 he is documented in Toledo; he also painted several important commissions in the city of Avila, including *retablos* for the Dominican church of Santo Tomás, and the *retablo mayor* for the Cathedral, unfinished at his death in 1504. But his hometown of Paredes de Nava was his professional base. The substantial number of altarpieces or surviving portions of them found in and around Paredes attests to activity there throughout his life; many of these works show assistance from his apparently large workshop.[3]

Along with Bartolomé Bermejo, Pedro Berruguete is considered the greatest of fifteenth-century Hispanic painters; he was certainly the greatest painter in Castile. Aside from the Osonas and their contemporaries in Valencia, he was one of the very few painters of his era to grasp the technical and compositional innovations of both Flanders and Italy.

The *Assumption of the Virgin* is one of nine surviving panels of a *retablo* dedicated to the Virgin Mary. The others include four narratives, the *Birth of the Virgin*, the *Annunciation*, the *Visitation*, and the *Death of the Virgin*, all from the altarpiece's body, and half-length Old Testament figures of *David*, *Solomon*, *Isaiah*, and *Jeremiah*, all from the *banco*.[4] The cult of the Virgin Mary thrived during the fifteenth century; indeed, more churches were dedicated to her than to anyone else during the medieval period, and more *retablos* contain scenes from her life, as well—particularly if her vital presence in the scenes of Christ's infancy is taken into account.

At least three *retablos* dedicated to the Virgin by Berruguete and his shop that include similar scenes and Old Testament figures are still found in and around Paredes de Nava. These include panels built into a later altarpiece found in the church of Santa Eulalia in Paredes itself, and another set originally from the church of Santa María, Becerril de Campos, but now in the church of Santa Eugenia in the same city.[5] The third set, with narratives of the life of the Virgin only, also came from Becerril de Campos, but is now in the Episcopal Palace in Palencia. Unfortunately, none of the groups of panels is still in its original configuration or frame, so it is impossible to speculate on their placement in their altarpieces. On the other hand, there are compositional similarities among them, suggesting that Berruguete and his workshop were producing these *retablos* according to a more or less standardized scheme, often reusing cartoons. It is, therefore, not surprising that the quality of painting among these sets of panels varies widely, according to the degree of shop intervention; those at Santa Eulalia are the best of the group.[6]

It is reasonable to assume that the *Assumption* and its accompanying panels came from an altarpiece from the same region, for while the theme of the Assumption is not represented among the surviving panels of the other altarpieces, other paintings in the group do repeat compositions found in the other *retablos*. Examples include the *Annunciation*, which can be compared to the *Annunciation* in the group now in the Episcopal Palace, and the Old Testament figures, which following Castilian custom, are half length and placed before gilded, brocaded grounds in all the surviving representations. As in the case of the other three *retablos*, the quality of execution also varies among the nine panels. The *Assumption* appears to be one of the panels in which Berruguete himself participated.

The *Assumption* is significant because it is a symbolic, rather than a narrative rendition of the story. There is no tomb, no surrounding apostles, no discernable setting—just the golden *mandorla* and the infinite blue of the setting. Though there is a crown above Mary's head, this painting is not a representation of the Coronation, for that subject would show the figure of Christ holding the crown, rather than angels, and both Mary and Jesus would be enthroned. Also, the Virgin stands on the crescent moon, an allusion to the Woman of the Apocalypse in the *Revelation to St. John* (12:1), which speaks of a woman clothed with the sun, with the moon under her feet, wearing upon her head a crown of twelve stars who becomes identified with the Virgin. The particular combination of all of these elements—the moon, a very concrete crown instead of an astral one, and the angels aiding in both the coronation and the levitation of the Virgin—is an early stage in the evolution of a theme which would become dear to the heart of Hispanic culture by

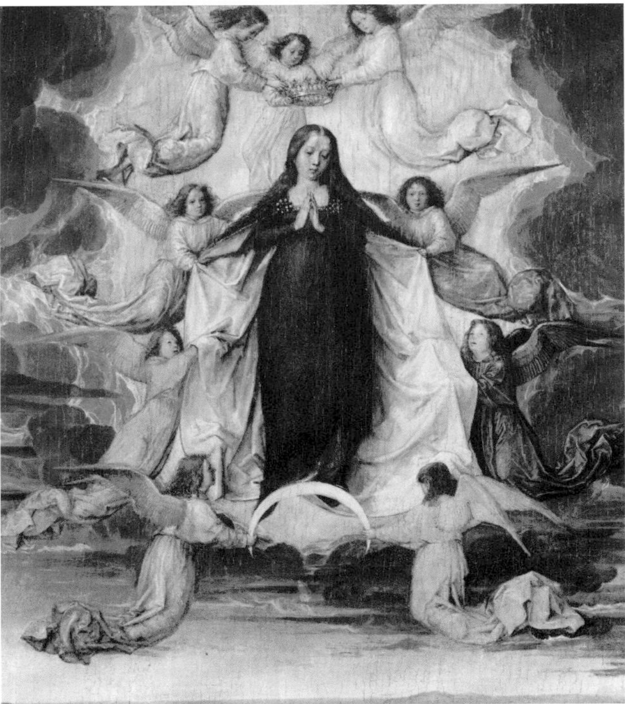

Figure 10-2

the seventeenth century: the Virgin of the Immaculate Conception.

We begin to see versions of this sort of *Assumption* during the last quarter of the fifteenth century. There is one, for example, in the *Polyptych of Queen Isabel* of 1496–1504, attributed to Michael Sittow (Washington, D.C., National Gallery of Art) (fig. 10-2), which is set in a dewy landscape, with nine angels instead of eight, and with the crescent moon turned down. The style of this panel is completely northern, even if the iconography is Iberian. Another contemporaneous Hispanic version is in a Castilian *retablo* originally in the church of Santa María de Arbás in Mayorga (fig. 10-3), and now in its new parish church. Here the ground is entirely gilded; the *mandorla* is fairly solid and has rays; and two angels hold the upturned crescent moon, two flank the Virgin, and two smaller ones hold her crown. This rendition also contains St. Thomas, who receives the Virgin's belt from her hands—added evidence that the iconographical context is not yet fixed.[7] Stylistically, Berruguete's *Assumption* and the other panels of the *retablo* from which it came fall somewhere in between these two works. Though there are some Netherlandish echoes in the floating garments of the angels, the vigorous figures themselves, with their pointed chins, aquiline noses, and broad brows are characteristic of Berruguete's distinctive style. On the other hand, the gold ground of the *mandorla* and the surface-oriented composition (in contrast to the deep space of the other Virgin narratives from the same altarpiece) are characteristically Iberian in character.

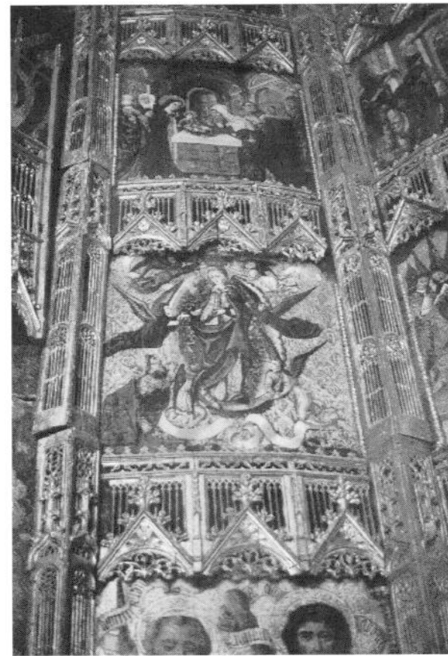

Figure 10-3

1. For complete biographical details on Berruguete, see the monograph by Federico Lainez Alcalá, *Pedro Berruguete, pintor de Castilla*, Madrid, Espasa Calpe, 1943.

2. The literature on Berruguete and the court of Urbino is voluminous. The most exhaustive proponent is still Chandler R. Post, *A History of Spanish Painting*, IX, Cambridge, Mass., 1947, 26–29. The lone skeptic is Federico Marías, *El largo siglo XVI*, Madrid, Taurus, 1989, 171–181.

3. The Catholic Kings, along with the Dominican Inquisitor Tomás de Torquemada, were among the principal contributors to the endowment of Santo Tomás in Avila. On the nature of Berruguete's patrons, see Joaquin Yarza, "Pedro Berruguete y su escuela," *Jornadas sobre el Renacimiento en la provincia de Palencia*, Palencia, 1987, 39–56, and Pilar Silva Maroto, "Notas sobre Pedro Berruguete y el retablo mayor de la catedral de Avila," *Anales de Historia del Arte* 1 (1989), 113.

4. All were in the collections of Raimondo and Luis Ruiz, which were broken up and sold in 1925. They are now scattered in different collections. See Eric Young, "A Rediscovered Painting by Pedro Berruguete and Its Companion Panels," *The Art Bulletin* 62 (1975), 473–475, for current locations and reproductions.

5. These are cited as being in Santa María by Post, 1947, 92–93, but their current situation is reported by Enrique Valdivieso González in Juan José Martín González, *Inventario artístico de Palencia y su provincia*, I, Madrid, Ministerio de Educación y Ciencia, 1978, 101.

6. There are even more panels from *retablos* on the theme of the Virgin from Berruguete and his shop than those cited here; they also included variations on a few basic compositions. See María Pilar Silva Maroto, "La iconografía como clave para una mejor comprensión de la personalidad de Pedro Berruguete," *Cuadernos de arte y iconografía*, 2nd semester, 1989, II, 6, 134–141.

7. The combination of Assumption and the giving of the belt to St. Thomas is rarely seen in Spain; it is far more prevalent in Italy, as in the famous example by Nanni di Banco on the Porta della Mandorla of the Cathedral in Florence. The entire *retablo* is illustrated in Judith Berg Sobré, *Behind the Altar Table*, Columbia, Mo., University of Missouri Press, 1989, plate 3.

Catalogue No. 11

ANONYMOUS CASTILIAN MASTER

Active in Salamanca(?), ca. 1490–1500

Tomb Figure of a Knight, ca. 1498–1500
Alabaster
17 x 76 x 37 3/4 in.
Isabella Stewart Gardner Museum, Boston
S6e14

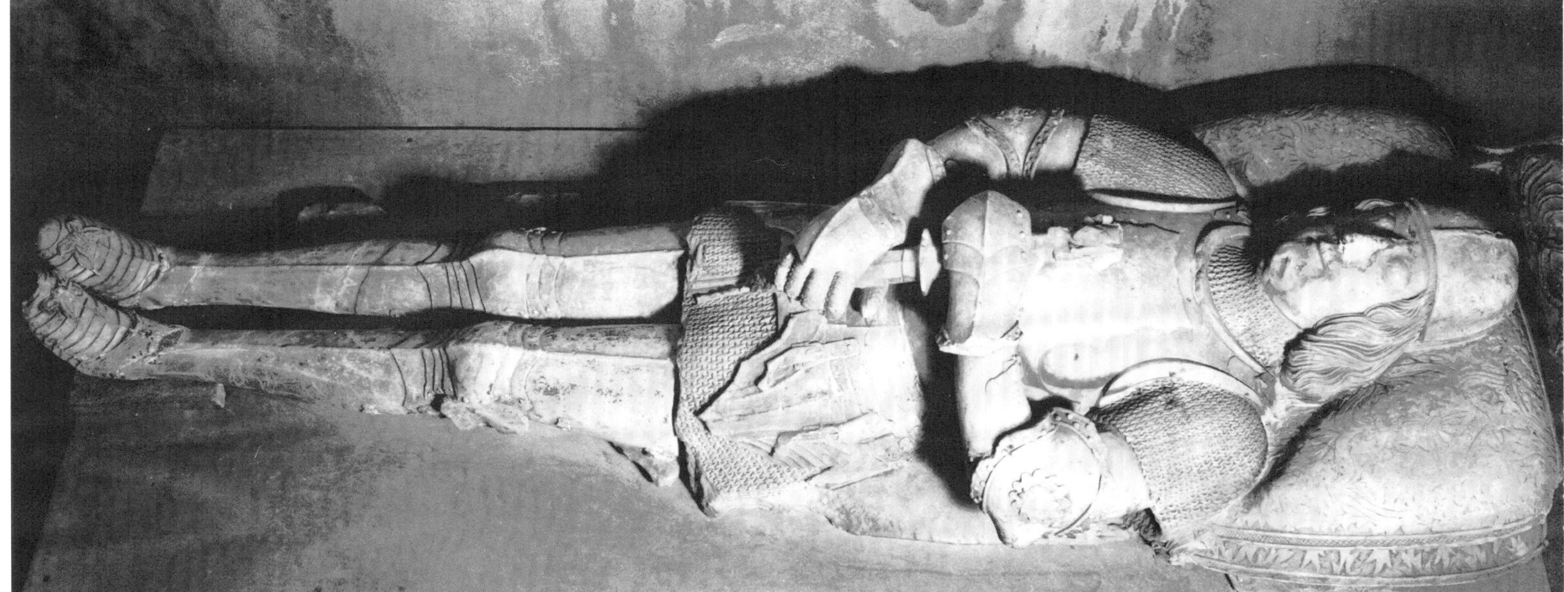

Figure 11-1

The somewhat squat and portly knight lies with his head on two pillows. He is dressed in full armor, including a chain-mail shirt, missing only his helmet. He grasps his sword in his two hands; the blade is now missing. His wavy hair is arranged in a page-boy style under a round cap prominently seamed in three places. Portions of the slab which would have formed the lid of his sarcophagus can be seen under his back and along his legs, which at some time were severed from his body and later rejoined, with the right leg broken in several places. The image must have been removed from its tomb with some violence, because the knight's nose was also broken off and subsequently reattached.

According to Emile Pares, who sold the piece to Isabella Stewart Gardner, the knight was a tomb effigy of a member of the Maldonado family, and it came from the city of Salamanca.[1] The Maldonados were members of Salamanca's aristocracy, though they were not particularly noteworthy in Spain's history. The exception was Dr. Rodrigo Arias de Maldonado, known as Dr. de Talavera, who was a Knight of Santiago, *Regidor* of Salamanca Cathedral, and who served on The Catholic Kings' Council (he was on the council that in 1486 turned down Columbus's request for funding for his initial voyage).[2] Dr. de Talavera founded a chapel in the Old Cathedral of Salamanca and was buried there in 1517, but many more of the Maldonado family were buried in the church of San Benito.

Among the Maldonado tombs in San Benito are those of Arias Peres de Maldonado and his wife, Elvira Hernàndez Cabeça de Vaca; Rodrigo Maldonado Monleon (died 1507); and Pedro Hernandez Maldonado.[3] All of these are wall tombs. The figures recline on top of their sarcophagi with their heads on double pillows set within decorated niches.

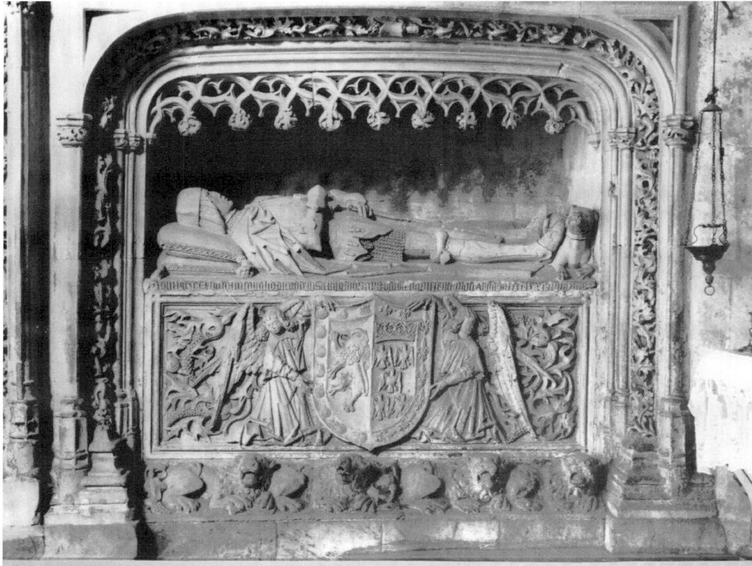

Figure 11-2

The gentlemen wear armor, with their helmets resting at their feet. The sarcophagi are embellished with elaborate coats of arms, heraldic lions, and, in the case of Arias Peres de Maldonado, Italian-style putti. This type of wall tomb and attendant decoration is typical of Salamancan production at the end of the fifteenth century and the first years of the sixteenth century.[4]

While there is no direct evidence other than the dealer's word that the *Tomb Figure of a Knight* truly represents a member of the Maldonado family (and perhaps was originally placed in a niche in the church of San Benito), the figure is close in conception to those still in the church. Though the hairstyle and cap are somewhat different from the known Maldonado tombs, the style of the armor is similar. It is also quite possible that a helmet could have been placed by the feet of the knight, much as helmets are in the Maldonado wall tombs. The figure would, of course, have to be imagined as being framed by a carved niche, with an elaborate coat of arms much like the others.

A possible date for the tomb figure is suggested by another tomb effigy from another noble family. It is the tomb figure of Ruberto de Santisteban, found in the Salamancan church of San Martín, who wears nearly identical armor and has a similar hairstyle and cap (fig. 11-2). Scholars date this tomb around 1500.[5]

Many attempts have been made to identify the knight more precisely. Records in the Gardner Museum identify this figure with the Comunard of Castile, no doubt a reference to Francisco Maldonado, who was executed for being one of the leaders in the revolt of the Comunidades against Charles I in 1521.[6] A more likely candidate chronologically would be yet another Rodrigo Maldonado, Lord of Barregas, who died in 1501, but bereft of a coat of arms or the context of a church, it is difficult to make further identification of the figure.[7]

1. Records of the Isabella Stewart Gardner Museum.

2. See Ferran Soldevila, *Historia de España*, III, Barcelona, Ediciones Ariel, 1962, 33 and 36, note 58.

3. Manuel Gómez Moreno, *Catálogo Monumental de España, Provincia de Salamanca*, I, Madrid, Ministerio de Educación y Ciencia, Dirección General de Bellas Artes, 1967, 229–230.

4. Agustí Duran I Sanpere, *Ars Hispanae, VIII: Escultura Gótica*, Madrid, Plus Ultra, 1956, 365.

5. Gómez Moreno, 1967, 170.

6. See Henry Kamen, *Imperial Spain, 1469–1714*, New York, Longman, Inc., 1983, 79. The Gardner records confuse Francisco with Pedro Maldonado.

7. Cornelius C. Vermeule III, Walter Cahn, and Rollin Van N. Hadley (*Sculpture in the Isabella Stewart Gardner Museum*, Boston, Trustees of the Isabella Stewart Gardner Museum, 1977, 146) point out that the device on the pillows is a pomegranate. The pomegranate is the symbol of the city of Granada, conquered by Fernando and Isabel in 1492, after which the device of the pomegranate was added to the Spanish coat of arms (see the coat of arms in this catalogue, fig. 12). Could the knight have participated in the conquest? If so, Rodrigo Maldonado might be a good guess, for he successively served Enrique IV of Castile and Fernando of Aragon.

Catalogue No. 12

ANONYMOUS

Royal Arms of the Catholic Kings, ca. 1493–1495
Iron
22 x 17 in.
Isabella Stewart Gardner Museum, Boston
M30e13

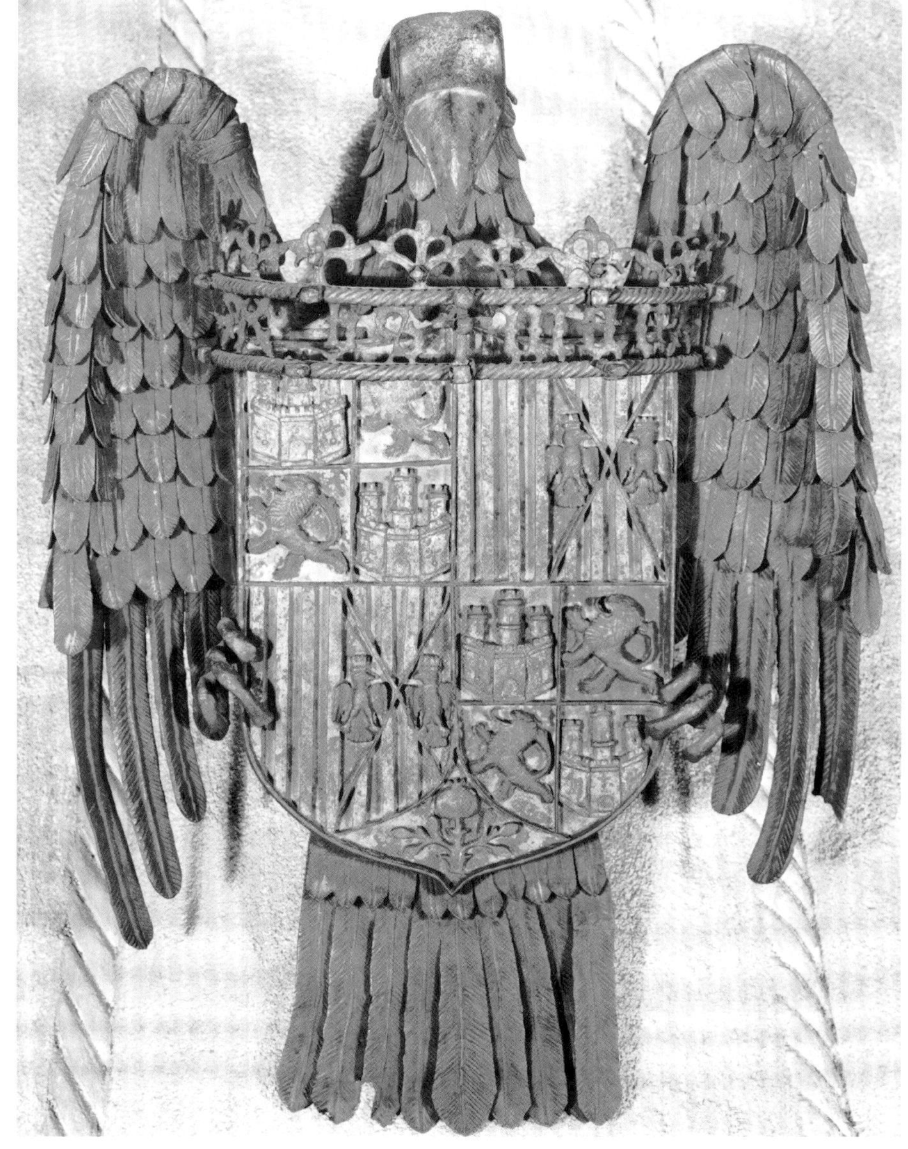

Figure 12

The coat of arms of the Catholic Kings itself is a standard rendition containing the combined arms of the Kingdom of Castile and León (castle and lion) and the Crown of Aragon (the four bars of Catalonia plus the bars and two crowned eagles of Aragon and Sicily) surmounted by an open crown. At the very bottom is the pomegranate, the symbol of the Nasrid Kingdom of Granada, conquered by the Catholic Kings in 1492, and then proudly added to their emblem. The arms are held between the claws of an eagle, symbol of St. John the Evangelist.[1]

The escutcheon comes from the Toledan church of San Juan de los Reyes, which was founded by the Catholic Kings. Both Fernando and Isabel were great patrons of religious art, founding and renovating a substantial number of churches, particularly those attached to monastic orders. San Juan de los Reyes was begun in 1476, to commemorate the monarchs' victory over the Portuguese fighting under King Afonso V. That victory was an important moment for Isabel, for she had had to fight for her claim to the crown of Castile. Isabel was the daughter of Juan II, and half sister of Enrique IV of Castile. Upon Enrique's death, in 1474, Isabel made a move to claim the throne, but so did Enrique's daughter, Juana. However, some question of Juana's legitimacy existed (rumor had it that the queen had had an affair with Beltrán de la Cueva, and that Juana was his child; Enrique was derogatorily known as the Impotent). Isabel wished to marry her cousin, Fernando, heir to the Crown of Aragon, for reasons both romantic and political. They did so in secret in 1469. In the meantime, Juana had become betrothed to Afonso V of Portugal, who eyed the Castilian throne covetously. Each side, of course, had powerful noble supporters. The two opposing factions met near the Castilian city of Toro in 1476, and Isabel's forces prevailed. It was the turning point in securing her succession, even though final settlement had to wait three years.

The Church of San Juan de Los Reyes, dedicated to John the Baptist, the patron saint of both Isabel's and Fernando's fathers, was founded as a Franciscan monastery church, with the idea that it would also become the royal pantheon for the rulers of the united kingdoms.[2] However, with the conquest of Granada, the royal pantheon was eventually established in the *Capilla Real* attached to that city's Cathedral. Nevertheless, San Juan de los Reyes was lavishly constructed under royal patronage by a succession of master builders of several nationalities, including Juan Guas, Simon de Colonia, Alonso de Yepes, and Alonso de Villaseca.[3] Construction proceeded rapidly, for by the time the German traveler Hieronymus Münzer visited Toledo in 1495, the church was largely complete, except for its choir and cloister.[4]

Pride in their royal establishment prompted the Catholic Kings to richly adorn San Juan's interior with sculptural decoration, including, in the crossing, a veritable frieze of the royal coat of arms, sustained by eagles, in a manner which has been likened both to tapestries and to Mudéjar ornament. These stone escutcheons lack the pomegranate of Granada and, therefore, must date to before 1492. The iron coat of arms seen here was probably executed to adorn a reja, or ornamental screen, ubiquitous in Spanish churches from the medieval period on. It is a common piece of Isabeline/Fernandine heraldry, for their arms were displayed on every structure they founded or patronized.

1. See Miguel Angel Ladero Quesada, "El proyecto político de los Reyes Católicos," *Reyes y Mecenas: Los Reyes Católicos, Maximiliano I y los inicios de la casa de Austria en España*, Madrid(?), Electa, 1992, 84.

2. Rosario Díez del Corral Garnica, "Arquitectura y magnificencia en la España de los Reyes Católicos," *Reyes y Mecenas,* 1992, 72.

3. Leopoldo Torras Balbás, *Ars Hispaniae: Arquitectura Gótica*, VII, Madrid, Espasa Calpe, 1952, 340.

4. Hieronymus Münzer, *Viaje por España y Portugal, 1494–1495*, Foreword by Manuel Gómez Moreno, trans. by José López Toro, Madrid, Colección Almenara, 1951, 130.

Catalogue No. 13

GIL DE SILOE

Active in Castile, 1486–1499

St. James the Greater, 1489–1493
Alabaster with traces of polychrome and gilding
18 x 7 x 5 3/4 in.
The Metropolitan Museum of Art
The Cloisters Collection, 1969
69.88

This small figure of the apostle St. James, patron saint of Spain, conforms to standard Iberian fifteenth-century iconography. He has long hair and a beard, and is dressed as a pilgrim with robe, cloak, hat, purse, and staff. The role of St. James as a pilgrim makes reference to the great shrine dedicated to him at Santiago de Compostela, one of medieval Christianity's three great places of pilgrimage (the two cockle—or scallop—shells, one on his hat, the other a pendant around his neck were the souvenirs that pilgrims to Santiago brought home with them as a symbol of their successful journey). Thus, James is depicted as a pilgrim to his own shrine!

The alabaster image was not meant to stand alone. It was originally part of the tomb of Juan II and Isabel of Portugal, which is still to be found (though somewhat altered) in the Carthusian Monastery of Miraflores, near Burgos (fig. 13-2).[1] This tomb is one of the most elaborate Hispanic funerary monuments of any period. Juan II founded the monastery in 1442, but the two royal tombs were not executed until considerably later. They were commissioned by Juan II's daughter, Queen Isabel, in 1486, and executed between 1489 and 1493.[2] The great ostentation and complexity of these tombs is more than a funerary homage of a daughter to her parents; it is clearly a political statement by Isabel, yet another public manifestation of the legitimacy of her dynastic claim to the throne of Castile similar to the one evident in the Toledan church of San Juan de los Reyes.[3]

The freestanding double tomb forms an eight-pointed star. It has effigies of the two monarchs reclining on pillows, though the canopies above their heads make them appear more like jamb figures on church facades: laid flat. Juan II holds his robe with one hand and raises the other, while Isabel holds an open prayer book; at their feet are lions. Surrounding them are a large number of small figures that include the Four Evangelists at the four cardinal points on top, saints on the subsidiary points and at the angles of the star, and, in niches below, Old Testament prophets and virtues (now somewhat altered and rearranged). This figure of St. James was originally one of the saints on the top. It was subsequently removed from the tomb and recycled into another monument, and at that time gilding and polychromy were added, for none was applied to the sculpture of the original tomb.[4]

The fine carving of the *St. James* gives only a little feeling for the complexity of execution of the entire tomb. Besides the many figures, there are borders of tracery, carved Gothic colonnettes, and niches. The two royal figures are the most astounding of all, for their garments are of rich brocade and jeweled ornaments; the detailing goes beyond tracery to filigree and pushes the art of stone carving to its limits.

The tomb is the documented work of Gil de Siloe and his workshop. Siloe, active in Spain from 1486, when he initially contracted for the royal tombs, is documented in Castile until 1499, working at Miraflores, Burgos, and Valladolid. Though several documents refer to him as French, scholars who have analyzed his style believe that he in fact came from the Netherlands or the Lower Rhine.[5] During the last half of the fifteenth century, the Kingdom of Castile was a virtual paradise for painters, sculptors, illuminators, and architects from many countries in Northern Europe, all patronized by a knowledgeable and cosmopolitan nobility. None was more knowledgeable and cosmopolitan than Queen Isabel, who, besides Siloe, employed at various times the architects Juan Guas from Brittany and Simon de Colonia (Simon of Cologne), the sculptor Egas Cueman from Brussels, and the painters Juan de Flandes (John of Flanders) and Michael Sittow (from Estonia); she also collected a sizeable number of northern paintings, tapestries, reliquaries, jewels, and illuminated manuscripts either through merchant intermediaries or directly from their sources.[6]

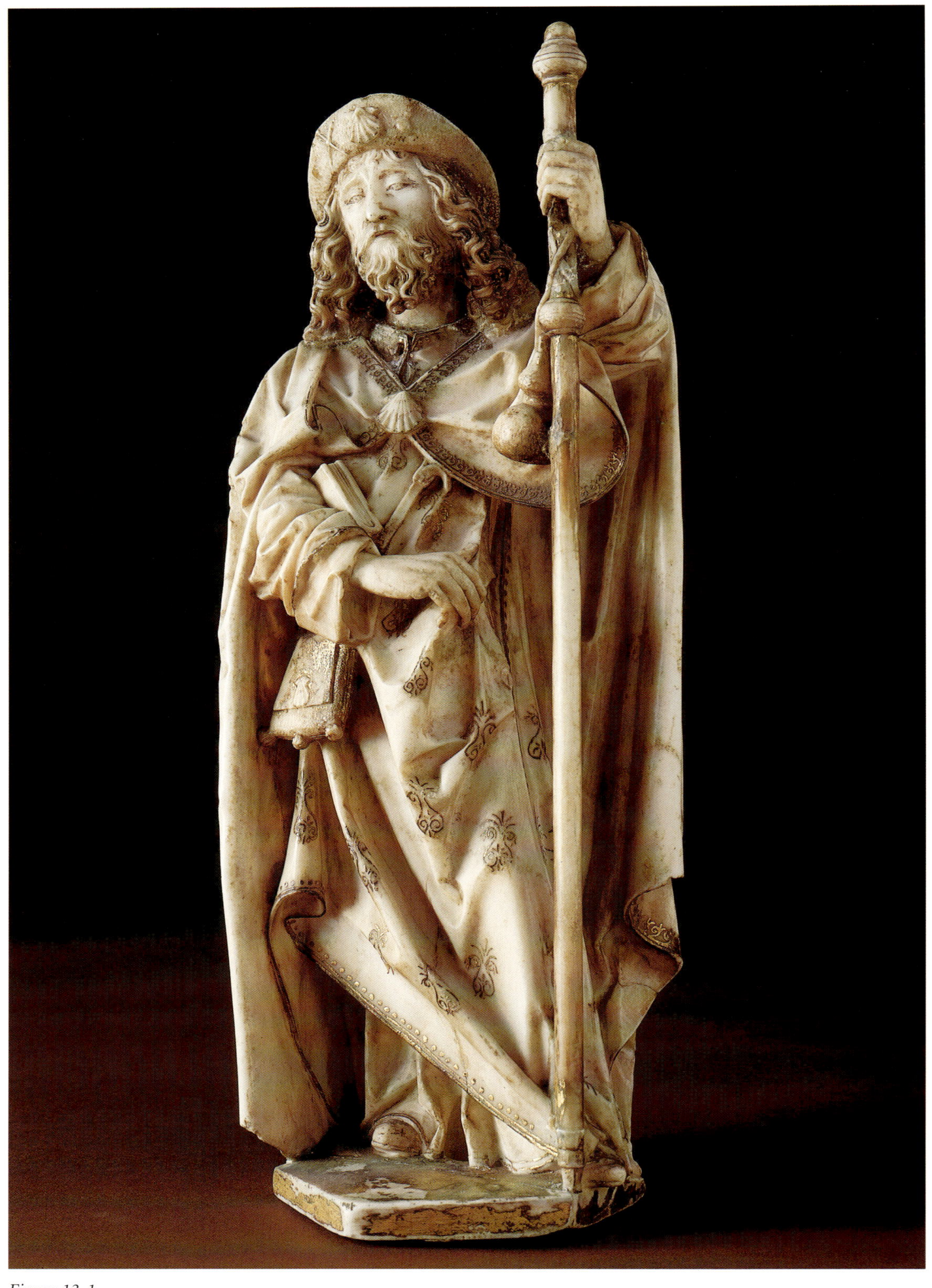

Figure 13-1

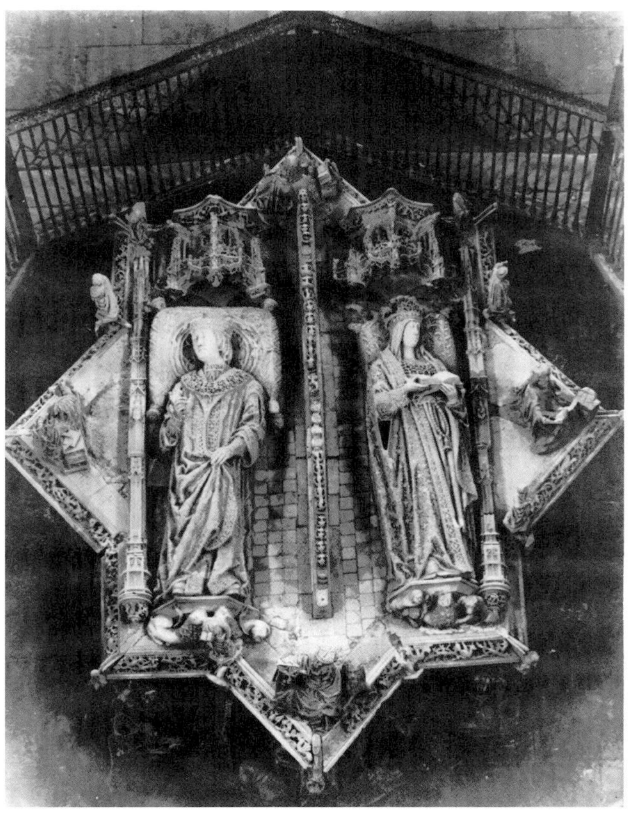

Figure 13-2

Though the origins of Siloe's style might be in the Netherlands, the general style of his tombs and great *retablos* conforms to the Isabeline aesthetic of late-fifteenth-century Castile, in which surfaces are virtually covered with a complex profusion of designs, so that individual figures are difficult to pick out. This surface complexity, along with the eight-pointed star that is the general shape of the joint tomb, are the manifestation of a subtle Mudéjar tradition in Castilian art that modifies whatever foreign currents form the style of individual figures. Exhibiting the figure of *St. James* alone provides the viewer the rare opportunity to contemplate the delicacy of the Siloe style in isolation, something that would not have been possible in the figure's original context.

1. For a history of the monument, see Harold Wethey, *Gil de Siloe and His School*, Cambridge, Mass., Harvard University Press, 1936, 31, 130.

2. Rhonda Kasl, "Gil de Siloe," in *Circa 1492, Art in the Age of Exploration*, ed. by Jay A. Levinson, Washington, D.C., National Gallery of Art, 1992, 166. Kasl's article is the definitive one on the *St. James*.

3. See the *Coat of Arms* of Isabel of Castile, fig. 12.

4. See Kasl, 1992, 166–167, for a discussion of the original arrangement and the question of polychrome and reuse. There were originally twelve saints. For another example of recycling of portions of a religious work, see fig. 4-1, Pere García de Benabarre, *St. Michael*.

5. Teófilo López Mata, *El Barrio e iglesia de San Esteban de Burgos*, Burgos, 1946, 103. Kasl, 1992, 166, cites one document that refers to him as French, while Jonathan Brown, "España en la era de las exploraciones: una encrucijada de culturas artísticas," *Reyes y Mecenas*, 117, note 8, cites another that describes him as a native of "urleones," which may be either Orléans or Lens.

6. See Francisco J. Sánchez Cantón, *Libros, tapices y cuadros que coleccionó Isabel la Católica*, Madrid, 1952.

Catalogue No. 14

BOOK OF HOURS, ROME-USE

Burgos(?), Segovia(?), Toledo(?), late 1470s (?)

Made for Don Alfonso de Castilla (1453–1468)(?), Isabel de Castilla (1452–1504)
Workshop of Juan de Carrión(?), active 1440s–1470s
Lent by the Pierpont Morgan Library, MS M. 854,
purchased with the assistance of the fellows, 1951
M. 854

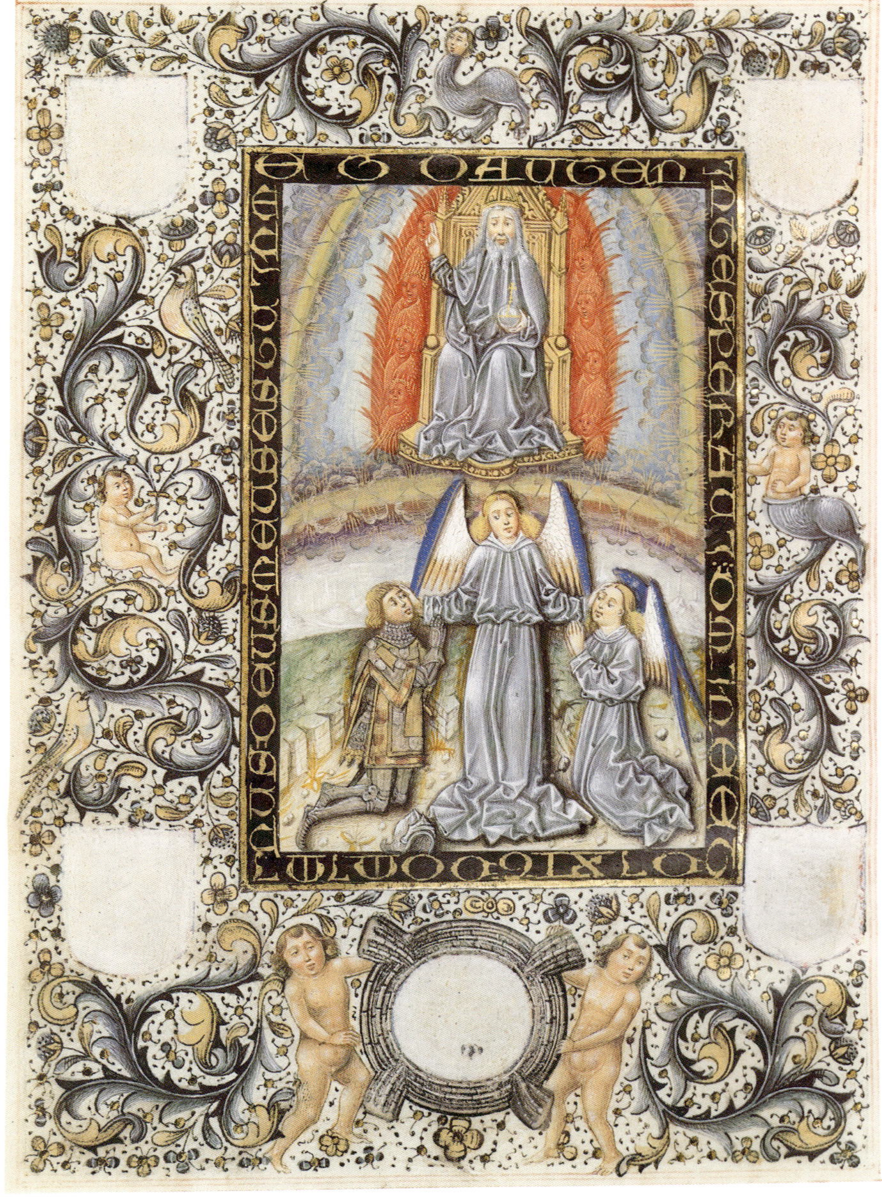

Figure 14

M. 854. This volume is comprised of 123 leaves of heavy, whitish vellum (225 x 160 mm), with modern numeration. Gatherings vary in number: 1(4); 2(1); 3(15); 4(11); 5(9); 6(9); 7(8); 8(8); 9(8); 10(8); 11(9); 12(11); 13(9); 15(13); 16(14); 17(9); 18(9); 19(11); 20(7); 21(15); 22(7); 23(10); 24(5); 25(10); 26(2); 27(2). Liturgical Gothic script, written in brown-black ink, 17 lines to a page (justification = 130 x 80 mm; Calendar justification = 130 x 90 mm also 17 lines to a page), ruled on red lines. Rubrics in red. Rebound in red morocco with gilding, Spanish eighteenth century, in marbled slipcase, broad dentelle borders enclosing the arms of Philip V of Spain (1683–1746), blue ribbon marker.

Text

ff. 1–2—blank
ff. 2v–14—Calendar (blank, but ruled and illuminated).
ff. 14v–15—blank.
ff. 16–19v—"*Incipit ordo dnica et comemoratio ad thronum domini.*"
ff. 20–21—blank.
ff. 21v–22—blank.
f. 22v—"*Incipit commemoratio Sci Iohannis Baptiste.*"
ff. 23–23v—Gospels.
ff. 24–24v—"*Incipit comemoratione Sci Iohanis Evangelisti.*"
f. 24v—blank.
ff. 25–33v—"*Passio dni secundum Iohanis Evangelisti.*"
f. 34—blank.
ff. 35–42v—Hours of the Cross.
f. 43—blank.
ff. 44–52v—Hours of the Trinity.
f. 53—blank.
ff. 54–121v—Hours of the Virgin.
  ff. 54–61v—Matins.
  ff. 63–79v—Lauds.
  ff. 81–84v—Prime.
  ff. 86–89v—Terce.
  ff. 91–94v—Sext.
  ff. 96–99v—Nones.
  ff. 101–107v—Vespers.
  ff. 109–121v—Compline.
f. 122—blank.
ff. 123–128v—Mass of the Virgin.
f. 129—blank.
ff. 130–134v—"*Obsecro Te*" (masculine).
f. 135—blank.
ff. 136–145v—Penitential Psalms.
ff. 146–147v—Litany of Saints, including St. Ildefonso of Toledo.
ff. 148–148v—Petitions.
ff. 149–153v—Psalms and Prayers.
f. 154—blank.
ff. 155–190v—Office of the Dead.
ff. 191–201v—Suffrages of the Saints, including Christopher, Catherine, Michael, and Ildefonso (f. 199—blank).
f. 202—blank
ff. 203–208v—Hours of the Sacrament.
f. 209—blank.
ff. 210–216v—Hours of the Holy Spirit.
f. 217—blank.
ff. 218–225v—Hours of All Saints.
ff. 226–232v—Hours of the Dead.
ff. 233–235v—Special Devotion to the Cross.
ff. 236–240v—Short Hours of the Virgin.

Illumination

Miniatures. Twenty-four full-page miniatures (approximately 130 x 80 mm); all leaves with miniatures are tipped in, with reverse side blank and unruled.

f. 1v—*St. Veronica.*
f. 15v—*Donor Portrait.*
f. 20v—*St. John the Baptist.*
f. 22v—*St. John the Evangelist.*
f. 34v—*Crucifixion.*
f. 43v—*Enthroned Trinity.*
f. 53v—*Annunciation.*
f. 62v—*Visitation.*
f. 80v—*Nativity.*
f. 85v—*Annunciation to the Shepherds.*
f. 90v—*Adoration of the Magi.*
f. 95v—*Presentation.*
f. 100v—*Massacre of the Innocents.*
f. 108v—*Flight into Egypt.*
f. 122v—*Virgin and Child.*
f. 129v—*Lamentation.*
f. 135v—*Last Judgment.*
f. 154v—*Raising of Lazarus.*
f. 163v—*Death.*
f. 199v—*St. Bernard of Clairvaux.*
f. 209v—*Pentecost.*
f. 212v—*Last Supper.*
f. 217v—*St. Ildefonso.*
f. 225v—*Mass of St. Gregory.*

Suffrage Illustrations

f. 191—*St. Christopher.*
f. 192—*St. Catherine.*
f. 193—*St. Michael.*
f. 194—*St. Andrew.*
f. 195—*St. Francis.*
f. 196—*St. Anthony.*
f. 197—*St. Sebastian.*
f. 198—*St. Ildefonso.*

Borders and Illuminated Letters
This manuscript has numerous pages with decorated borders. The borders are composed of curving, thick sprays of acanthus, stylized carnation and strawberry plants, aroid buds, star and trefoil flowerettes, flowers with multiple petals, and seed pods. Many pages include interlaced knots, hairline stems, and vases in the border decoration. In addition to the phyllomorphic elements, the borders also feature putti, angels, birds, monsters, animals, courtiers, and disembodied heads. The Calendar illustrations represent the Zodiac and the Labors of the Months.

Provenance
This manuscript was owned by a citizen of Valladolid, according to a note on the flyleaf ("*Por mandado y comisión de los ilustres señores inquisidores de Valladolid fueron estas horas vistas y examinadas por mi Fray Nicolás Ramos*"). Ramos left Spain in 1599 to become archbishop of Puerto Rico; the manuscript remained in Spain. Later, it entered the collection of Philip V, king of Spain. In 1894, it was owned by the comte des Lignerolles. Baron Jean Vitta acquired it in 1929. The Morgan Library purchased it from Baron Vitta in 1951.

Books of Hours, like this one (hereinafter called M. 854), were produced in western Europe from the Middle Ages into the Renaissance.[1] These manuscripts were owned by the rich bourgeois, or by aristocrats, who used them for private devotions. The content of Books of Hours could vary, but they all contained the text for the celebration of the Office of the Blessed Virgin Mary, which included the recitation of specific prayers, psalms, and hymns at each of the canonical hours (matins, lauds, prime, terce, sext, nones, vespers, and compline). Frequently, Books of Hours were richly illuminated. M. 854 is one of the finest illuminated manuscripts produced in western Europe. The content of Books of Hours often varied according to the wishes of their owners, who could choose to include favorite saints, prayers, offices, or special commemorations to reflect their personal devotional practices. The variety of personal choices made by medieval and Renaissance patrons meant that each Book of Hours was a unique creation.

Books of Hours were also written to be used regionally. The inclusion of local saints, offices, or prayers associated with specific churches, towns, cities, or countries helps to localize a Book's intended place of use. M. 854 was written according to the use of Rome, which means that it conformed to the rite of the Roman Catholic Church as practiced in the Renaissance.[2] In many instances, the Calendar of a Book of Hours can also be used to localize the manuscript's intended place of use because calendars frequently include the celebration of feasts of saints of local importance. Unfortunately, M. 854 has a blank Calendar, thereby making localization difficult. Previous scholarship has suggested the city of Toledo as the place of manufacture for this Book of Hours, a suggestion that is supported by the inclusion of St. Ildefonso in the Litany of Saints and in the Suffrages of the Saints.[3] It is true that St. Ildefonso was especially venerated in Toledo, but he was also generally venerated throughout Castile. Therefore, his presence in this Book of Hours alone is not a secure indicator for Toledan localization.[4]

Traditionally, M. 854 has been considered to have been written and illuminated for Don Alfonso de Castilla, the younger brother of Isabel de Castilla, who died in 1468, at the age of fifteen. The arms that appear in the *bas-de-page* of folio 34v (there shown supported by two angels) are the arms of Castile—a gold castle with three turrets on a field of red. On folio 15v, the arms have been defaced, but the comte des Lignerolles recorded that their original appearance corresponded to those seen on folio 34v.[5] Their mutilation postdates Lignerolles's ownership, yet predates Baron Vitta's acquisition, as the arms were already destroyed when he purchased the book. [6] The miniature on folio 15v represents a blond youth dressed in a coat of chain mail decorated with a border composed of the arms of Castile and León. The youth's appearance corresponds to contemporary descriptions of Don Alfonso de Castilla, who was the heir to both kingdoms, hence it is suggested that he was the patron.

Additional support for this supposition is found in the inclusion of a portrait of a blond queen in the miniature of *Death* found on folio 163. Erwin Panofsky drew attention to this miniature by convincingly identifying it as a portrait of Isabel de Castilla.[7] The presence of the queen is not explained by Panofsky despite the questions it raises. In the miniature, the unidentified queen wears a crown, yet Isabel was not queen of Spain until her coronation in 1474, six years after her brother's death.[8] During Don Alfonso's lifetime, Isabel was second to him in the line for the throne and she would not have been entitled to the crown.

Another puzzling detail visible in the *Death* miniature is the inclusion of the figure of a young armored knight among the dead—was this knight intended to be understood as the deceased Don Alfonso? If the dead youth is Alfonso and the crowned queen is his sister, Isabel de Castilla, then the manuscript could in whole, or in part, postdate 1468, the year of Alfonso's death. It could also, given the presence of the crown, postdate Isabel's coronation. It is even possible that the manuscript was begun for Don Alfonso and then completed for Isabel, in a consistent style, some years later. Or, perhaps, the manuscript was commissioned by Isabel in memory of her brother after she was crowned.

The illumination of M. 854 is similar to that of the Book of Hours of Juana Enriquez, a manuscript attributed to the Flemish workshop of Wilhelm Vrelant.[9] As Juana Enriquez was the mother of Fernando de Aragon, Isabel's husband,

and as Isabel acquired this manuscript from her mother-in-law, the resemblance in the style of illumination between these two manuscripts could indicate a later date for M. 854, as Isabel did not marry Fernando until 1469, a year after her brother's death.

While the illumination of M. 854 resembles that of the Book of Hours of Juana Enriquez, it does not resemble the style of illumination in manuscripts that can be securely localized to Toledo.[10] A link does exist between M. 854 and two other Spanish manuscripts—a Missal, dated 1476, written and illuminated for Cardinal Pedro González de Mendoza (Archive of the Cathedral of Toledo, Ms. Res. 5) and a matching Breviary (Library of the Monastery of El Escorial, Ms. b.III.16), also made for the cardinal.[11] The Missal made for Mendoza has a half-page miniature representing the *Crucifixion* on folio 119.[12] The artist responsible for this miniature also painted the *St. John the Baptist* of M. 854. Unfortunately, the Missal and Breviary made for Mendoza cannot be localized. Some indicators in the text and in the illumination of the Mendoza manuscripts suggest manufacture in Burgos, Segovia, or Seville, but as these links are diverse, a secure localization is not possible.[13] The date of 1476, found on folio 8 of the Missal, suggests a contemporaneous date for M. 854's decoration, as the style of the Missal's *Crucifixion* and that of M. 854's *St. John the Baptis*t is very close.

The illumination of M. 854 is the work of four artists. One was responsible for the illumination of the Calendar and the miniatures accompanying the Suffrages of the Saints. A second artist, the same one responsible for the *Crucifixion* in the Mendoza Missal, contributed the *Donor Portrait*, the *St. John the Baptist*, and possibly, the miniature of *St. John the Evangelist*. The third artist painted the *St. Veronica*, the *Last Judgment, the Death*, the *Last Supper*, the *Pentecost*, the *St. Ildefonso*, and the *Mass of St. Gregory*. The remaining miniatures were the work of a fourth artist.

Almost every page of this manuscript has marginalia, executed in a dark *grisaille* tone complemented only by touches of subdued coloration. The same tonality is maintained in the miniatures. The style of this decoration was linked by T. J. Brown, G. M. Meredith-Owens, and D. H. Turner to another Book of Hours in the collection of the British Library, which had been previously attributed to a Toledan workshop.[14] The manuscript to which M. 854 has been linked (British Library, Add. 50004) is the first half of a Book of Hours; the second part is in Berlin (Kupferstichkabinett, Berlin-Dahlem Museum, A78A26).[15] The Office of the Blessed Virgin Mary is identical in the two books, suggesting that they were intended to be used in the same place.

The British Library/Berlin manuscript is not, in fact, the product of a Toledan workshop; rather, its style indicates that it is a product of the workshop of the Castilian miniaturist Juan de Carrión. Juan de Carrión's workshop was, at different times in his career, located in Guadalajara (where he worked for the Mendozas, whose family palace was located in that city), Segovia, and Avila. Although the *grisaille* tones of M. 854 are not usual in manuscripts attributed to the Carrión workshop, the general configuration of space, figural types, and the content and arrangement of the marginalia are similar enough to indicate kinship.

Given the textual and stylistic correspondences, it can be suggested that M. 854 should be linked to the Carrión workshop. Hence, it is possible to consider M. 854 as having been manufactured in one of the northern Castilian cities in which the Carrión workshop was active. The Carrión workshop was in Guadalajara only until 1455, the year of the death of its patron in that city, Don Iñigo López de Mendoza, marqués de Santillana. It is likely that M. 854 was commissioned later, while the workshop was in Avila working on the choirbooks for the Cathedral, which were completed by 1472.[16] It is also possible that M. 854 was made in Segovia, where the Carrión workshop enjoyed royal patronage from Enrique IV de Castilla.[17]

It is suggested here that M. 854 is a Book of Hours perhaps commissioned for Don Alfonso de Castilla before his death, but possibly completed for Isabel de Castilla soon after her brother's death, in 1468, but also after her coronation, in 1474. The correspondence between the manuscript's style and that of the Carrión workshop during the late 1470s supports a later date for the manuscript. A later date is also indicated by the appearance in M. 854 of the artist responsible for the Mendoza Missal's *Crucifixion*. These suggestions are not intended to be conclusive, but they do recast the traditional consideration of this Book of Hour's context.

1. For a general description of Books of Hours and their content, see Roger S. Wieck, *Time Sanctified: The Book of Hours in Medieval Art and Life*, New York, George Braziller, 1988. The author thanks Julie Roth for her assistance with the manuscript entries.

2. For a discussion of specific rites and feasts, see Andrew Hughes, *Medieval Manuscripts for Mass and Office: A Guide to Their Organization and Terminology,* Toronto, 1982.

3. For a description of the textual content of M. 854, see Lynette M. F. Bosch, "Manuscript Illumination in Toledo (1446–1482): The Liturgical Books," Ph.D. diss., Princeton University, 1985, 514–519.

4. For other cities where Ildefonso was venerated, see Bosch, 1985, 187–315.

5. Comte R. L. de Lignerolles, *Catalogue des libres rares et précieux*, Paris, 1894.

6. M. 854 has also been described and discussed by Paul Durrieu, "Manuscrits d'Espagne rémarquables par leurs peintures et par la

beauté de leur execution," *Bibliothèque de l'Ecole des Chartes* 54 (1893), 300; Jesús Domínguez Bordona, *Exposición de Códices Miniados Españoles,* Barcelona-Madrid, 1929, 130–131; Jesús Domínguez Bordona, *La Miniatura. Ars Hispaniae*, Madrid, 1962, vol. 18, 211; New York, Pierpont Morgan Library, *Treasures from the Pierpont Morgan Library, Fiftieth Anniversary Exhibition*, New York, 1957, 23; John Plummer, *Liturgical Manuscripts*, New York, 1964, 47–48; New York, Pierpont Morgan Library, *Major Acquisitions 1924–1974: Medieval and Renaissance Manuscripts,* New York, 1974, no. 41.

7. Erwin Panofsky, *Early Netherlandish Painting*, New York, 1953, 349.

8. On Isabel de Castilla, see Peggy K. Liss, *Isabél, the Queen*, New York/Oxford, 1992; and Nancy Rubin, *Isabella of Castile: The First Renaissance Queen*, New York, 1992.

9. On Vrelant, see James Douglas Farquhar, *Creation and Imitation*, Fort Lauderdale, 1976, 103–112, and see 103–112 for a description of the Hours of Juana Enriquez.

10. On Toledan illumination, see Bosch, 1985.

11. On these manuscripts, see ibid., 515–535.

12. On the significance of this miniature, see Lynette M. F. Bosch, "*A terminus ante quem* for two of Martin Schongauer's *Crucifixions*," *The Art Bulletin* 64:4 (1982), 633–635.

13. The indicators of links to these cities are discussed in Bosch, 1985, 515–517.

14. See T. J. Brown, G. M. Meredith-Owens, D. H. Turner, "Manuscripts from the Dyson Perrins Collection," *The British Museum Quarterly* 23:2 (1961), 27–38.

15. For a discussion of the workshop of Juan de Carrión, to which this manuscript can be attributed, see Lynette M. F. Bosch, "Los Manuscritos Abulenses de Juan de Carrión," *Archivo Español de Arte*, 253 (1991), 55–64; idem, "Iluminación en Avila y Segovia Durante el Siglo XV: Los Libros Litúrgicos del Grupo de Juan de Carrión," *Archivo Español de Arte*, Madrid, 256 (1991), 472–487 and idem, "El Taller de Juan de Carrión: Los Libros Seculares," *Archivo Español de Arte*, 264 (1993), 353–371.

16. The payment documents for the Avila choirbooks were published by María Silva Maroto, "La Miniatura Hispano-flamenca en Avila: Nuevos Datos Documentales," *Miscelánea de Arte*, 1982, 55–56.

17. See Bosch, 1993, 356–361, 362.

Catalogue No. 15

ST. AUGUSTINE OF HIPPO, *DE CIVITATE DEI* ("ON THE CITY OF GOD")

Toledo, 1446–1455(?)

Made for Archbishop Alfonso Carrillo de Acuña, archbishop of Toledo (1446–1482)

Illumination attributed to Cano de Aranda

The Metropolitan Museum of Art

Gift of Mary LeRoy

X430.1–3, three volumes, one exhibited

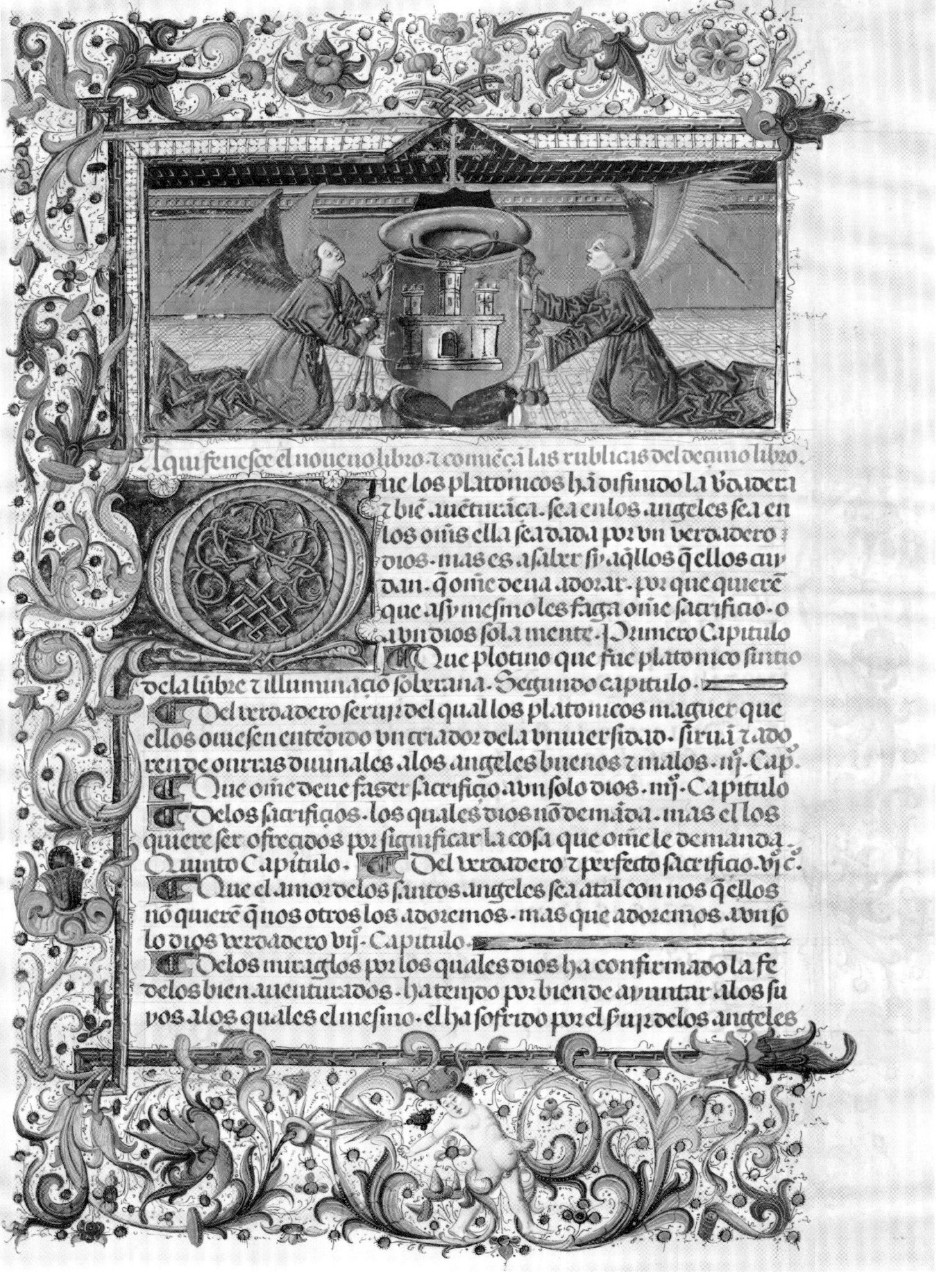

Aqui fenesçe el noueno libro 7 comiẽçã las rublicas del deçimo libro.
Que los platonicos hã difinido la vdadera
7 biẽ auẽturãça. sea enlos angeles sea en
los omẽs ella sea dada por vn verdadero
dios. mas es a saber si aq̃llos q̃ ellos ay
dan. q̃ omẽ deua adorar. por que quierẽ
que asy mesmo les faga omẽ sacrifiçio. o
a vn dios sola mente. Primero Capitulo
Que plotino que fue platonico sintio
dela lunbre 7 illuminaçiõ soberana. Segundo capitulo.
Del verdadero seruir del qual los platonicos maguer que
ellos ouiesen entẽdido vn criador dela vniuersidad. siruiã 7 ado
ren de onrras diuinales alos angeles buenos 7 malos. iij. Cap.
Que omẽ deue faser sacrifiçio a vn solo dios. iiij. Capitulo
Delos sacrifiçios. los quales dios nõ demãda. mas el los
quiere ser ofreçados por significar la cosa que omẽ le demanda.
Quinto Capitulo. Del verdadero 7 perfecto sacrifiçio. vj. c.
Que el amor delos santos angeles sea atal con nos q̃ ellos
nõ quierẽ q̃ nos otros los adoremos. mas que adoremos a vn so
lo dios verdadero vij. Capitulo.
Delos miraglos por los quales dios ha confirmado la fe
delos bien auenturados. ha tenido por bien de ayuntar alos su
yos alos quales el mesmo. el ha sofrido por el seruir delos angeles

Figure 15

X430.1. This volume is comprised of 316 leaves of thick, yellowish vellum (425 x 285 mm), with modern numeration. Gatherings of six throughout, although the original gatherings were of ten, as is indicated by the catchwords. Pages have been cut. Two leaves (blank, but ruled) were added to the front, one to the back.

X430.2. This volume is comprised of 244 leaves of thick, yellowish vellum (425 x 285 mm), with modern numeration. Catchwords indicate gatherings of ten. Two leaves (blank, but ruled) were added in front and back; rebound into gatherings of six.

X430.3. This volume is comprised of 252 leaves of thick yellowish vellum (425 x 285 mm), with modern numeration. Catchwords indicate gatherings of ten, except for one blank (ruled) back leaf; rebound into gatherings of six. Liturgical Gothic script, written in brown-black ink, with chapter headings in red, 35 lines to a page (justification = 230 x 160 mm), ruled on blue lines, with the two upper and two lower vertical and horizontal rulings extended to the edges of the page. Original binding of reddish brown leather, blind-tooled with a Mudéjar pattern. The original binding was retained when the manuscript was rebound and two blank, unruled, paper leaves were added (one in front, one in back). The leaves lack watermarks.

Text

The text of St. Augustine's *City of God* was translated from the original Latin into Spanish, with a commentary by the Spanish translator.

X430.1

ff. 1–1v—Table of Contents.
ff. 1v–25— Book I.
ff. 25–26—Table of Contents.
ff. 26–48—Book II.
ff. 48–49—Table of Contents.
ff. 49–73—Book III.
ff. 73–74v—Table of Contents.
ff. 75–97v—Book IV.
ff. 97v–98v—Table of Contents.
ff. 98v–128—Book V.
ff. 128–129—Table of Contents.
ff. 129–152—Book VI.
f. 152—Table of Contents.
ff. 152–155v—Book VII.
f. 156—Table of Contents.
ff. 156–216v—Book VIII.
ff. 216v–217v—Table of Contents.
ff. 217v–244—Book IX.

X430.2

f. 1—Table of Contents.
ff. 2–47v—Book X.
ff. 48–48v—Table of Contents.
ff. 48v–78—Translator's Prologue. Book XI.
ff. 78–79v—Table of Contents.
ff. 79v–102—Book XII.
ff. 102–102v—Table of Contents.
ff. 103–124v—Book XIII.
f. 125—Table of Contents.
ff. 125–159 —Book XIV.
ff. 159–160v—Table of Contents.
ff. 160v–216—Book XV.
f. 216—Table of Contents.
ff. 217–273v—Book XVI.
ff. 274–274v—Blank.
f. 275—Table of Contents.
ff. 275–316—Book XVII.

X430.3

ff. 1–2v—Table of Contents.
ff. 3–75v—Book XVIII.
ff. 75v–76—Table of Contents.
ff. 76–118v—Book XIX.
f. 118v—Table of Contents.
ff. 119–163v—Book XX.
ff. 164–206v—Book XXI.
ff. 206v–208—Table of Contents.
ff. 208–252—Book XXII.

Illumination

X430.1. On folio 3v one illuminated initial within which there is a representation of St. Augustine, enthroned, dressed in bishop's regalia (jeweled mitre, pink cloak, white alb, green stole), with his right hand raised in blessing as he holds a crozier in his left.

X430.2. On folio 1 one half-page miniature, depicting a room with a tiled floor that recedes in one-point perspective towards a brick wall. In the foreground, two angels bear the arms of Archbishop Carrillo surmounted by the green, archbishop's hat. The page is surrounded by a decorative border.

X430.1–3. All three volumes have numerous pages with decorated borders and illuminated initials.

Provenance

The Metropolitan Museum's Medieval Department acquired this manuscript after 1932. A notice from an unidentified sales catalogue is preserved in the Museum's records: "*Augustín (Sancto) De la Cibdad de Diós con Exposición de Traslador sobre los capítulos.* 3 vol. Magnificent manuscript by a first-rate Spanish scribe, Exquisitely ornamented with 7 beautiful miniatures (the first exhibiting St. Augustin seated on his throne), 20 large initials, 1000 capital letters, 891 superb floriated borders, in which are introduced figures of angels, peacocks and other birds, children, male and female heads, St. George and the dragon, monkies, etc. In the highest style of early art, oak boards covered in stamped leather saec. XIV–XV probably executed for a Cardinal of Castilla or Aragón, as his arms (a castle) are painted beneath the portrait of St. Augustin and on the reverse of the leaf these arms were those of Cardinal Peter de Luna [this is an error], before being the AntiPope Benedict XIII. The miniaturist was probably a Spanish pupil of an Italian artist [this is also erroneous]."

Augustine of Hippo (354–430) was born in Tagaste (Souk-Akras, Algeria) and died in Hippo. His father, Patricius, was a pagan; his mother, Monica, was Christian. Early in his life, Augustine studied rhetoric and law at Madaurus and Carthage. He was strongly interested in Manichaeism and Plotinian Platonism, as well as in the writings of Cicero and the philosophy of Aristotle. After his baptism in Milan on Easter Sunday of 387, he began to attempt to merge the philosophy of the Greeks with Hebraic and Christian religious beliefs. In so doing, he created a transcendental philosophical system based on Platonic metaphysics. In 391, he became a priest, and in 395, he was elevated to the rank of bishop of the Church.

De Civitate Dei was written between 413 and 427. In it, Augustine developed the metaphor of the two cities—the Heavenly City of God and the Worldly City of Earth. Augustine wrote *De Civitate Dei* as a defense of Christianity, following the fall of Rome to Alaric, the Visigoth, in 410. The fall of Rome to Alaric, who was a Christian, was seen by many in the city to be a judgment against them for having abandoned their pagan deities. Augustine maintained in this work that Alaric had come to purify Rome with the new Christian order.

The Metropolitan Museum's Spanish translation of *De Civitate Dei* was commissioned by Archbishop Alfonso Carrillo de Acuña, archbishop of Toledo from 1446 to 1482. Carrillo's arms appear on folio 1 of X430.2, and on folios 2v and 3 of X430.1.[1] The manuscript's illumination is the work of three artists.[2] The artist responsible for the illumination of folios 1, 1v, 10, and 10v of X430.2 can be identified as Cano de Aranda, the miniaturist who signed his name to two Toledan manuscripts also made for Archbishop Carrillo. These manuscripts are both Missals. One is in the Archive of the Cathedral of Toledo (Ms. Res. 4) and the other is in the British Library (Add. 38.037). The second miniaturist illuminated folios 11–39 and 102–252 of X430.3. The third miniaturist painted the initial with St. Augustine in folio 3v of X430.1, as well as the rest of the illumination found in the three manuscripts.

The manuscript dates from the earlier years of Carrillo's tenure, as it was then that Cano de Aranda illuminated the two Missals for him.[3] The style of the decoration of the Metropolitan's manuscript exhibits features that are characteristically Toledan, such as the use of scrolled acanthus, hairline stems, aroid buds, flowerettes, leafy flowering plants, gold seed-dots, birds, animals, and putti.

1. For a description of this manuscript see Lynette M. F. Bosch, "Manuscript Illumination in Toledo (1446–1482): The Liturgical Books," Ph.D. diss., Princeton University, 1985, 580–585.

2. For a discussion of the illumination found in this manuscript and its connections to Toledan illumination, see Lynette M. F. Bosch, "Una Nueva Atribución a Cano de Aranda, Miniaturista Toledano," *Archivo Español de Arte*, 249 (1990), 69–79.

3. See Bosch, 1985, 555–558.

Catalogue No. 16

EGIDIO ROMANO (GUIDO DELLE COLONNE OR GILES OF ROME), *DE REGIMINE PRINCIPIUM*

Guadalajara, 1435–1455

Made for Don Iñigo López de Mendoza, marqués de Santillana (1398–1455)

Illumination attributed to Jorge Inglés

Gift of Philip Hofer in memory of Thomas Stilwell Lamont, Department of Printing and Graphic Arts

Houghton Library, Harvard University

fMS Typ 195

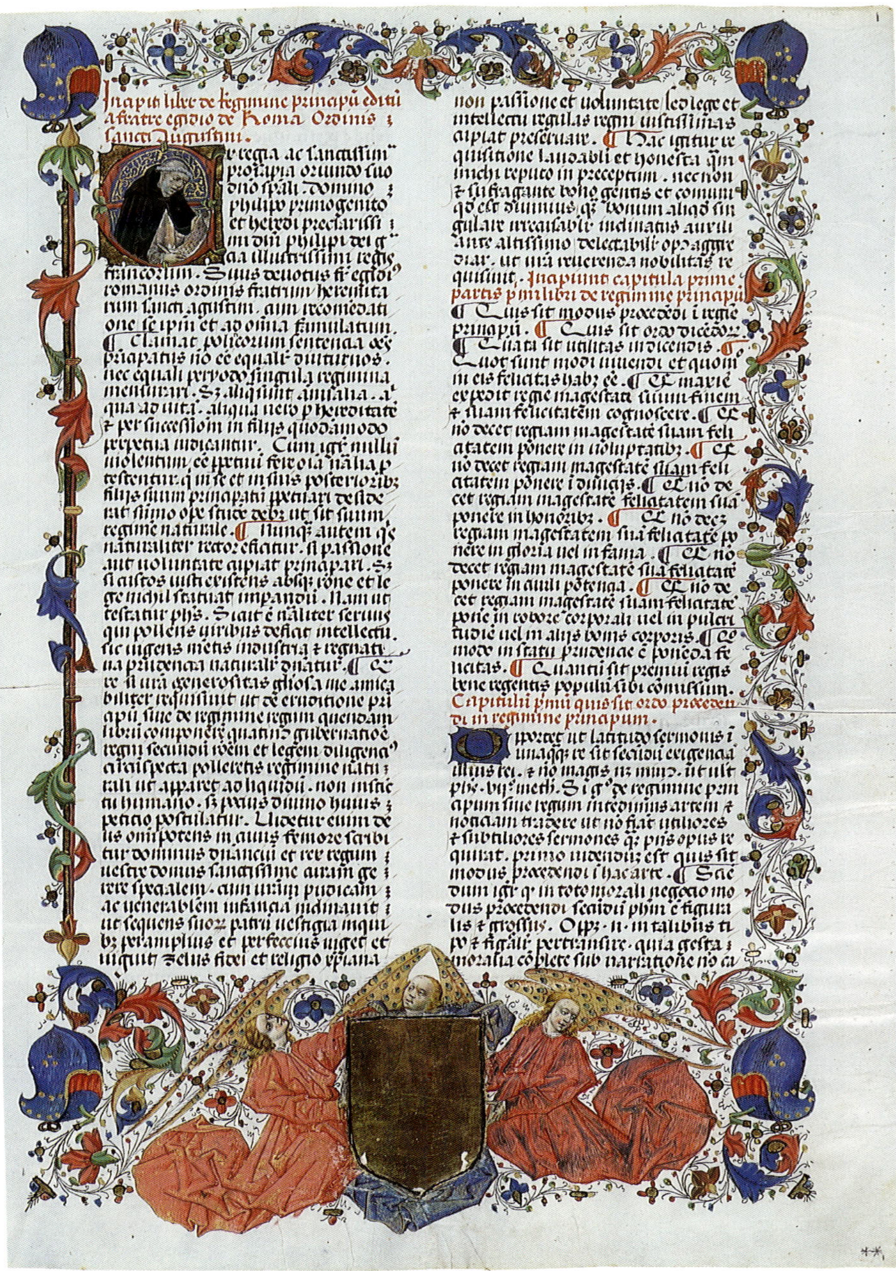

Figure 16

fMS Typ 195. This volume is comprised of 130 leaves of thin, whitish vellum (308 x 224 mm), with modern numeration. Gatherings vary in number: 1(2) blank, unruled; 2(12); 3(12); 4(12); 5(6); 7(7); 8(6); 9(4); 10(12); 11(6); 12(14); 13(5); 14(12); 15(12); 16(10); one blank leaf at the end, unruled. Spanish cursive script, written in brown-black ink. Double-columns of text throughout (52 x 208 mm), 51 lines (justification = 150 x 208 mm). Red/blue calligraphic initials throughout. Ruled in silverpoint. Original Mudéjar binding of reddish brown, tooled leather, with gilt edges.

Text

The text is in Latin and reproduces Egidio Romano's *De Regimine Principium.*

Illumination

Folio 1. Title page decorated with a pseudoportrait of the author found in the initial "E," which begins the text. Border decoration surrounds the text and is composed of acanthus, hairline stems, flowerettes, aroid buds, and gold seed-dots. In the four corners, four helmets. In the *bas-de-page*, a shield is supported by three angels. The shield lacks arms and has only the burnished gold background on which the arms would have been painted.

Provenance

The manuscript's original owner appears to have been Don Iñigo López de Mendoza, marqués de Santillana (1398–1455). It was in the collection of the duke of Osuna (Plut. II. Lit. N, no. 6). From there, it passed into the collection of George Dunn and that of E. P. Goldschmidt. It was purchased by Philip Hofer from Goldschmidt in 1953 and presented, in 1982, to the Houghton Library.[1]

Egidio Romano (Guido delle Colonne), also known as Giles of Rome, archbishop of Bourges, was a member of the Roman Colonna family. He was a medieval theologian and philosopher. Born in Rome, ca. 1243, he died in Avignon on December 22, 1316. Early in life, Egidio joined the *Eremitani di Sant' Agostino* and went to Paris to study. He is important for his contributions to political philosophy, among which the *Regimine Principium* is a leading work. The text of this book explains Egidio's political philosophy, which can be simply understood to have centered around the concept that if kings and princes put their faith in God, He will guide them to correct actions.

The helmets that appear in the four corners of the decorative border painted on folio 1 were the personal device of Don Iñigo López de Mendoza, marqués de Santillana.[2] Santillana was a bibliophile, who between 1435 and 1455 amassed a personal library of approximately one thousand books. This was a remarkable accomplishment considering that the papal library at Avignon possessed only twice that number. Santillana was a soldier, a courtier to Juan II de Castilla and to Enrique IV de Castilla, and, most significantly, one of Spain's leading Renaissance poets. He was also the head of the powerful and aristocratic family of the Mendoza.[3]

As a bibliophile, Santillana collected the same type and variety of texts that were sought after by other fifteenth-century collectors:[4] works from classical antiquity, theological treatises, biblical texts and commentaries, and late medieval and Renaissance poetic allegories. Guido delle Colonne's *Regimine Principium* would have complemented the library's holdings.

The attribution of the border to Jorge Inglés was made by Chandler R. Post to Philip Hofer.[5] It was based on Post's acceptance of F. J. Sánchez Cantón's attribution of a series of manuscripts which are now in the Biblioteca Nacional de Madrid to Jorge Inglés, and on the similarity of the angels found in those manuscripts to the ones decorating this manuscript's folio 1.[6] Sánchez Cantón's attribution of the illumination was based on a stylistic comparison of the angels that appear in those manuscripts holding up the arms of Santillana and the angels that appear in the *Retablo de los Angéles*, an altarpiece originally intended for the high altar of the hospital church of Buitrago. The *Retablo de los Angéles* is documented by the codicil added to Santillana's will on June 5, 1455, which allocates funds for the completion of the altarpiece, "*el de los angéles*," to "*Jorge Inglés*." The design and content of folio 1's border conform to those that appear in the manuscripts previously attributed to Inglés, and there is a strong similarity between the angels seen in this manuscript and those of the *Retablo de los Angéles*. While it may not be possible to securely attribute this illuminated page to Inglés, it is certainly a product of the workshop to which he belonged.

1. Roger S. Wieck, *Late Medieval and Renaissance Illuminated Manuscripts (1350–1525) in the Houghton Library*, Cambridge, Mass., 1983, 98–99, where previous bibliography is assembled.

2. Wieck, 1983, 98.

3. See Helen Nader, *The Mendoza Family in the Spanish Renaissance* (1350–1550), New Brunswick, N.J., 1979.

4. Mario Schiff, "La Bibliothèque du marquis de Santillane," *Bibliothèque de l'Ecole des Hautes Etudes*, fasc. 153, Paris, 1905.

5. Wieck, 1983, 98.

6. F. J. Sánchez Cantón, "Maestro Jorge Inglés, pintor y miniaturista del Marqués de Santillana," *Boletín de la Sociedad Española de Excursiones* 25 (1917), 99–105, and 26 (1918), 27–31.

Catalogue No. 17

MOSES BEN MAIMON (MOSES MAIMONIDES)

Mishneh Torah
Toledo, 1260
Scribe, Moses ben Joseph Amarillo
From the Felix Friedman Collection. Presented by a group of donors in 1951.
Houghton Library, Harvard University
Ms. Heb. 36

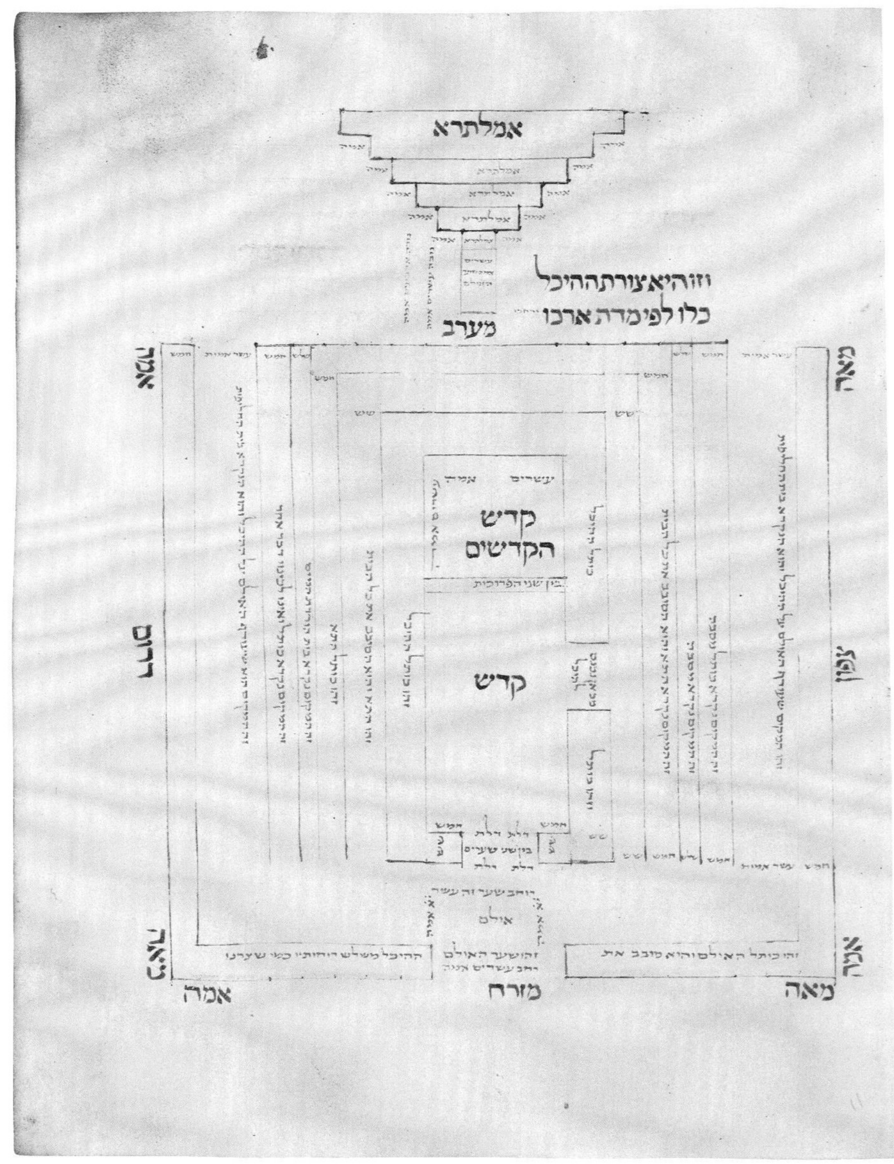

Figure 17

Ms. Heb. 36. This volume is comprised of 209 leaves of heavy, whitish vellum (312 x 237 mm), with modern numeration. Gatherings vary throughout: 1(6); 2(10); 3(6); 4(10); 5(6); 6(8); 7(8); 8(8); 9(8); 10(7); 11(10); 12(3); 13(7); 14(7); 15(9); 16(9); 17(7); 18(7); 19(7); 20(13); 21(9); 22(6); 23(10); 24(6); 25(6); 26(4); 27(5); 28(3); 29(6); 30(6), with one white paper leaf at the end (blank, unruled). Square script, written in brown-black ink, 27 lines to a page (justification = 125 x 225 mm). Pages were cut down and mutilated, probably to remove illuminated borders and initials. Modern binding of green/brown marbled paper.

Text

The text conforms to that of Moses ben Maimon's *Mishneh Torah: Avodah, Korbanot.*

Provenance

The original owner of the manuscript was Judah ha-Rofe ben Moses ha-Kohen, as is stated in the colophon on folio 159v. It passed eventually into the collections of Simkhah Pinsker and Felix Friedman, until it was given to the Houghton Library at Harvard University in 1951.[1]

As stated in the colophon on folio 159v, this manuscript was written by the scribe Moses ben Joseph Amarillo for its original owner, Judah ha-Rofe ben Moses ha-Kohen. The text reproduces Moses ben Maimon's (Moses Maimonides) *Mishneh Torah.* The manuscript was made in Toledo, and it is a fine example of the production of Hebrew manuscripts in Spain. The manuscript has been greatly mutilated, as the margins and tops of pages throughout have been cut off. Probably, these mutilated pages were originally illuminated. The illumination would have been removed to be sold separately in modern times.

Although most illuminated manuscripts made in Spain were Christian, manuscripts like this *Mishneh Torah* would have been manufactured for Spain's Jewish population. The history of the fortunes of the Jews in Spain is mixed, as they enjoyed periods of relative peace and prosperity alternating with periods of persecutions and pogroms. The life of Moses ben Maimon is typical of the Jewish experience in Spain.

Moses ben Maimon (Rabbi Mosheh ben Maimon, RaMBaM) was born in Córdoba, ca. 1135, and died in Cairo, in 1204. He was born into a scholarly family that encouraged his intellectual interests, which eventually led to his study of the Talmud. In 1148, his family fled Spain to escape persecution at the hands of Islamic fundamentalists. The family went to southern Spain, then North Africa, where they settled in Fez. From there, they traveled to Morocco and Israel, eventually settling in Fustat (Old Cairo). There, Maimonides became the house physician to Saladin's vizier and the untitled leader of the Jewish community.

While performing his duties as a physician, Maimonides began writing his treatises on the central areas of Jewish law (*halakhah*). His most important works are: *Perush ha-Mishnah* (Commentary on the Mishnah); *Sefer ha-mitsvot* (Book of the Commandments); *Mishneh Torah*, or, *Yad ha-hazaqah* (Review of the Torah); and *Moreh Nevukhim* (Guide of the Perplexed). He also wrote ten medical treatises based on Arabic writings on medicine. The *Mishneh Torah* (Study of Torah) was written as an introduction to aid a review of the Talmud. It is a fourteen-volume code of law that took from 1158 to 1168 to complete. It remains a work that is crucial to Jewish thought, for it contains unique perspectives on Jewish religious philosophy and law as well as a definition of the term "Israelites" and the formulation of the thirteen articles of faith that every Israelite is expected to endorse. The *Mishneh Torah* was written in the Hebrew of the Mishnah, rather than in the Hebrew of the Bible, or the Aramaic of the Talmud, so that it could be read by a general reader. The square script in which this version of the *Mishneh Torah* is written accords with the spirit of the language used, as it is the style of Hebrew script that is the most accessible. The illumination, which most likely once decorated this script, indicates that the manuscript was commissioned for private use, as graven images would not have been permitted in a manuscript meant for use inside a temple.

The diagram that appears on folio 11 of this manuscript is a floor plan and elevation of the Temple of Jerusalem. The text of folios 10–12 describes the physical appearance of the Temple and the illustration gives visual form to the words of that description. The diagram is inscribed with words and numbers that identify the different parts of the Temple and of the complex site on which it was built. At the top of the page, the words "Ceiling Beam" and "Cross Beam/Rafter" appear with words indicating height measurements: "Forty" and "Twenty Cubits." The word "Foundation" is included along with such notations as, "This is the height of the hidden meeting hall," and "This is the shape of the Temple of the Ark of Law in the Synagogue, all according to the measurements of the length and the width. The height is twenty cubits."

The floor plan is annotated "West" (above, center), "South" (left), "North" (right), and "East" (bottom, center). In the corners of the plan, the words "Cubits" and "One Hundred" alternate. The center text states "Holy of Holies," and below that the word "Holy" appears. Around the perimeters of each of the inside sections are the measurements of the widths of the walls: "Five," "Ten," "Five," "Three," "Five," "Six," and "Six." Below the east side is the Gate, identified with the words "This is the gate of the auditorium, its width is twenty cubits," and "The width of the gate is Ten." In the center, the word for "Auditorium/Meeting

Hall" appears, alongside this text: "This is the wall of the auditorium and it surrounds the Temple from its three winds like our gate." Another entryway existed in the north, as is indicated by the words "Entry to the Temple is in the North." On the north side of the plan appear these words: "This is the place where the overflow of the Auditorium is, and it is the house of health/sanity/healing." Next to this text, are the words "This is the place called the wall of reception/gathering." The walls are described ("Wall of the Temple" and "This is a Wall") and the interstices in between the walls are also described ("This is the place called compartment and it surrounds the whole house" and "This the place called the gathering"). On the south side are written: "This is the wall of the Temple. This is the compartment and it surrounds the whole house"; "This is the place called the house of bringing down the water"; "This is a place called wall, and it doesn't have any specific name"; and "This is the place where the overflow of the Temple is."

The accompanying text is descriptive. On folio 10, it describes a part of the temple as follows: "From the north to the south—one hundred cubits—the width of the wall to the auditorium is five cubits. From the wall of the auditorium to the wall of the Holy of Holies is ten cubits. The walls of the Holy are six cubits and in between them five empty spaces between the outer wall and between the two." Hence, by reading the text and following the diagram, the reader could reconstruct the appearance of the Temple.

1. Mordechai Glatzer, *Hebrew Manuscripts in the Houghton Library of the Harvard College Library*, Cambridge, Mass., 1975, 10–11, Moses ben Maimon, (1135–1204) Mishneh Torah: Avodah, Korbanot, Ms. on vellum: Toledo, 1260, 220f. (439 p.), 31.2 x 23.7 cm, square script. In the hand of Moses ben Joseph Amarillo (colophon f. 159v). The author thanks Deborah Huacuja for translating the Hebrew text.

Catalogue No. 18

PEREZ BEN ISAAC HA-KOHEN (FOURTEENTH CENTURY)

Ma'arekhet ha-Elohut

Sepharad(?), fifteenth–sixteenth century(?)
Presented by a group of donors in 1951
Houghton Library, Harvard University
Ms. Heb. 60

Ms. Heb. 60. This volume is comprised of 132 leaves of whitish parchment (220 x 150 mm), with modern numeration. Gatherings vary: two blank, unruled, leaves at the front; 1(10); 2(10); 3(18); 4(16); 5(10); 6(16); 7(9); 8(14); 9(10); 10(10); 11(7); two blank, unruled, leaves at the back. Rabbinic script, written in yellowish-brown ink, 24 lines to a page (justification = 78 x 125 mm). Modern binding of brown, marbled paper.

Text

ff. 1–32v—Ma'arekhet ha-Elohut.
ff. 33v–36v—Jacob bar Sheshet, excerpt from Meshiv devarim nekhohim.
ff. 36v–38v—Ot ha-alef-me-ha-ketuvim.
ff. 39–47—Perush, Merkevet Yehezkelel.
ff. 47v–51—Sefer Yetsirah.
ff. 51v–77v—Sefer ha-bahir.
ff. 77v–125v—Midrash ha-ne'elam. (Zohar hadash) Li-megilat Rut. Midrash Rut.
ff. 125v–132v—Menahem Recanati, Perush ha-tefilot.

Provenance

The manuscript was in the collection of Felix Friedman until it was given to the Houghton Library at Harvard University by a group of donors in1951.[1]

The *Ma'arekhet ha-Elohut* is attributed to Perez ben Isaac ha-Kohen (Cohen, Gerondi), who lived toward the end of the thirteenth century. He is known to have been the author of cabalistic treatises. This manuscript is written in rabbinic script and in the Hebrew of the Bible as well as in the Aramaic of the Talmud. The use of rabbinic script indicates that it was intended for a scholarly audience rather than for reading by the general populace. The *Ma'arekhet ha-Elohut* is a tract that expounds a system for achieving godlines or holiness.

The second treatise found in this compendium is a series of excerpts from the *Meshiv devarim nekhohim* of Jacob bar Sheshet. Its text sets forth the protocols for the act of listening to correct things. This text is followed by the *Ot ha-alef-me-ha-ketuvim*, which is a mystical discussion of the sacred significance of the letter *alef.* The *Perush, Merkevet Yehezkelel* is an explanation of the significance of the Chariot of Ezekiel. The *Sefer Yetsirah* is an explanation of the Book of Creation. The *Sefer ha-bahir* is a Book of Enlightenment. It is followed by the disappearing Midrash (a secret work), or the *Midrash ha-ne' elam.* Following this is the *Zohar hadash*, or the New Zohar, which is a compendium of mystical writings. The *li-megilat Rut* is a transcription of the scroll that tells the story of Ruth. It is followed by the *Midrash Rut*, where an explanation is given for the story of Ruth with a focus on the lessons to be learned from the story. The *Perush ha-tefilot* of Menahem Recanati is an explanation of the meaning of prayers.

Manuscripts of this nature would not have been illuminated, as they were not intended for general use, and their illumination would have violated the prohibition against graven images. Their value resided in the text, and they were commissioned and prized for the wisdom they contained.

1. Mordechai Glatzer, *Hebrew Manuscripts in the Houghton Library of the Harvard College Library,* Cambridge, Mass., 1975, 18.

Catalogue No. 19

ANONYMOUS CRAFTSMAN
Active in Nasrid Kingdom of Granada

Fragment of a Textile
Second half of fourteenth century
Silk and metallic-wrapped silk
20 1/8 x 8 11/16 in.
The Textile Museum
Acquired by George Hewitt Myers in 1931
84.5

The motifs on this fragment are arranged in an overall repeat pattern of interlaced Kufic script (Arabic) with a single word, Allah (God), repeated and reversed and depicted as a series of braided characters, with floral ornament, immediately under and framed within pairs of split palmette leaves forming arches arranged in staggered rows. A thin line of red silk woven on the gold ground outlines the designs executed in white green and blue, the latter two confined to the foliage and arabesques, the white to the arches.

The decorative motifs used here directly reflect tile and stucco work in the Alhambra, particularly in the Palacio de los Leones built under Sultan Muhammad V (1362–1391). The style of the Kufic inscription further bears this out.[1]

Fine Islamic weaving had a long history in Spain, dating back to the earliest days of the Caliphate of Córdoba, and continuing through the Taifas, Almoravid, and Almohad periods. It was basically a courtly craft, and many of the best textiles were extremely luxurious, even during the relatively austere period of Almohad domination, and frequently included inscriptions. They were used for ceremonial court garments and diplomatic gifts. Metallic thread was often used, as well as fine silk. The decorative motifs are characteristic of Nasrid weaving, as is the metallic wrapping of yellow silk to intensify the effect of the gold thread.

In earlier periods, Christians prized these when they could get them, for a sizable number of these luxury textiles were either directly ordered by them for garments or else captured and recycled into the liners of reliquaries and tombs. They were also used for vestments, following the Iberian medieval custom of explicitly recycling the products of one religion's culture into the other for their own use. By the Nasrid period, textiles were a major export product.[2]

Iberian Christians (and Jews, for that matter) were thoroughly comfortable with Islamic decorative aesthetic and language and incorporated much of them into their own products.

1. See the commentary of Florence Lewis May, *Silk Textiles of Spain,* New York, The Hispanic Society of America, 1957, 146. Regarding this fabric, May observes "A development of this design may be seen as part of the stucco wall decoration in the Halls of Comares and of The Two Sisters in the Alhambra Palace."

2. Palma Martínez Burgos, in *Reyes y mecenas. Los Reyes Católicos, Maximiliano I y los inicios de la Casa de Austria en España*, Madrid, Electa, #32, 303.

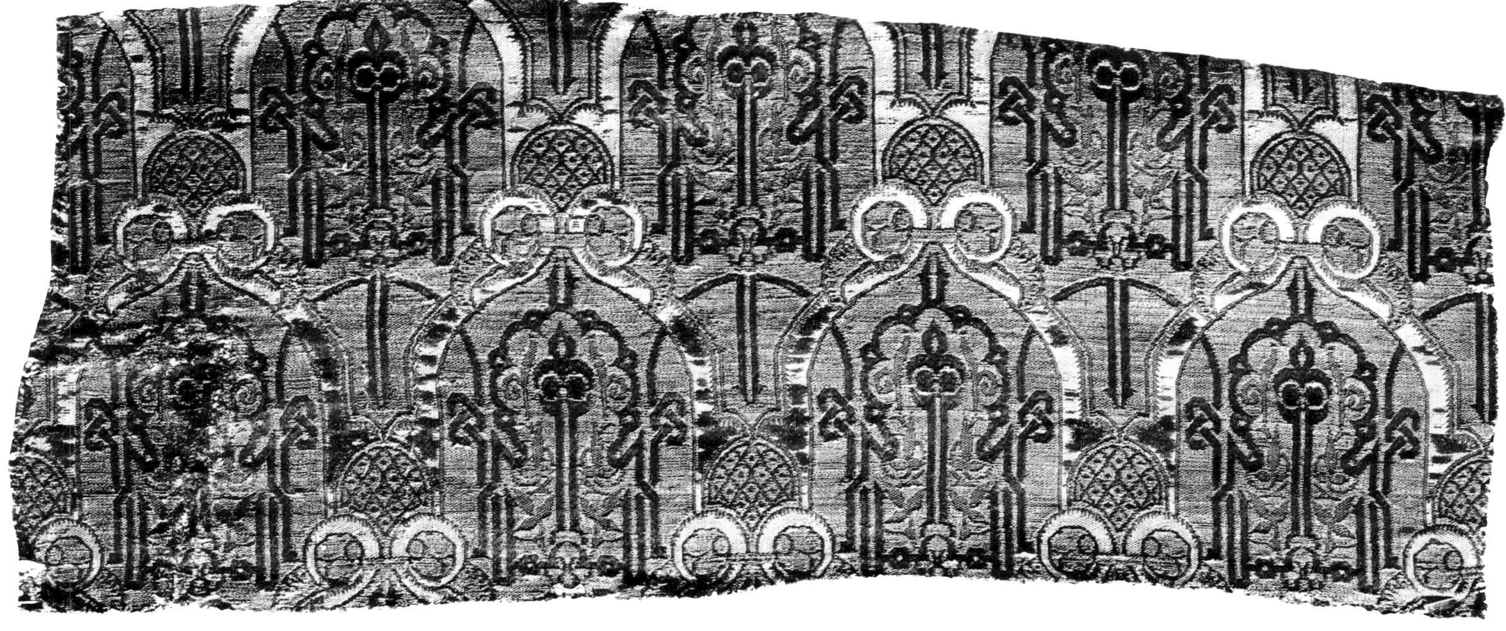

Figure 19

CHECKLIST OF THE EXHIBITION

1a) Bartolomé Bermejo
(active in various cities in Aragon, ca. 1468–1495)
St. Engracia, ca. 1475
Oil on conifer panel
64 1/4 x 28 1/2 in.
Isabella Stewart Gardner Museum, Boston
P19e25

1b) Bartolomé Bermejo
The Capture of St. Engracia, ca. 1475
Oil on conifer panel
43 x 26 in.
San Diego Museum of Art
Gift of Misses Anne R. and Amy Putnam
1941:101

2) Martín Bernat
(active in Zaragoza, 1469–1497)
St. Blaise Enthroned, ca. 1480
Oil and gold leaf on panel
53 3/4 x 38 1/8 in.
Colnaghi, London and New York

3) Francesc Comes
(active in Mallorca, 1392–1415)
The Virgin and Child, Sts. George, Martin, and Anthony Abbot, ca. 1395
Tempera and gold leaf on panel
29 9/16 x 45 1/8 in.
Isabella Stewart Gardner Museum, Boston
P16e16

4) Pere García de Benabarre
(active in Catalonia and eastern Aragon, 1445–1483)
St. Michael, after 1461
Tempera and gold leaf on panel
72 x 56 in.
Isabella Stewart Gardner Museum, Boston
P19s7

5) Gonçal Peris de Sarrià
(active in Valencia, 1380–1451)
St. Lucy, ca. 1425
Egg tempera and some oil on conifer panel
56 1/8 x 36 5/8 in.
Williams College Museum of Art
Gift of Karl E. Weston, Class of 1896, in memory of Ruth Sabin Weston
54.2

6) Circle of Rodrigo and Francesc de Osona
(active in Valencia, 1463–1518)
Agony in the Garden, ca. 1490
Oil on panel
7 9/16 x 6 3/16 in.
Museum of Art, Rhode Island School of Design
Mary B. Jackson Fund
57.282

7) Anonymous Mudéjar Craftsman
(active in Manises)
Bowl with the Arms of Aragon and Sicily, ca. 1465
Metallic glazed ceramic
18 7/8 in. (diameter)
The Minneapolis Institute of Arts
The Christina N. and Swan J. Turnblad Memorial Fund, 1962
62.11

8) Anonymous Andalusian Master
Virgin and Child with Female Saint and St. Jerome, ca. 1465
Tempera, oil, and gold leaf on panel
20 3/8 x 13 3/4 in.
The Metropolitan Museum of Art
The Friedsam Collection
Bequest of Michael Friedsam, 1931
32.100.105

9) Master of the Catholic Kings
(active in Castile, ca. 1495–1500)
The Presentation in the Temple
Oil on panel
62 x 38 in.
Fogg Art Museum
Harvard University Art Museums
Francis H. Burr Memorial Fund and Anonymous Gifts
1933.29

10) Pedro Berruguete
(active in Castile, 1477–1504)
The Assumption of the Virgin
Oil and gold leaf on panel
56 x 36 in.
Davis Museum and Cultural Center
Wellesley College
Gift of Mr. and Mrs. A. M. Adler
1965.52

11) Anonymous Castilian Master
(active in Salamanca (?), ca. 1490–1500)
Tomb Figure of a Knight, ca. 1498–1500
Alabaster
17 x 76 x 37 3/4 in.
Isabella Stewart Gardner Museum, Boston
S6e14

12) Anonymous
Royal Arms of the Catholic Kings, ca. 1493–1495
Iron
22 x 17 in.
Isabella Stewart Gardner Museum, Boston
M30e13

13) Gil de Siloe
(active in Castile, 1486–1499)
St. James the Greater, 1489–1493
Alabaster with traces of polychrome and gilding
18 x 7 x 5 3/4 in.
The Metropolitan Museum of Art
The Cloisters Collection, 1969
69.88

14) Attributed to the Workshop of Juan de Carrión
Book of Hours, Rome-Use, late 1470s(?)
Open to folio 15v, *Donor Portrait*
Made for Don Alfonso de Castilla(?)
Lent by the Pierpont Morgan Library (MS M. 854), purchased with the assistance of the fellows, 1951
M. 854, f. 15v.

15) Attributed to Cano de Aranda
St. Augustine of Hippo
De Civitate Dei ("On the City of God")
Made for Archbishop Alfonso Carrillo de Acuña, archbishop of Toledo (1446–1482)
Open to folio 1, half-page miniature of two angels holding Archbishop Carrillo's arms
The Metropolitan Museum of Art
Gift of Mary LeRoy
X430.1-3, three volumes, X430.2 exhibited

16) Attributed to Jorge Inglés
Egidio Romano (Guido delle Colonne or Giles of Rome)
De Regimine Principium
Made for Don Iñigo López de Mendoza, marqués de Santillana (1435–1455)
Open to folio 1, frontispiece, showing the collection marks of the marquis of Santillana
Gift of Philip Hofer in memory of Thomas Stilwell Lamont, Department of Printing and Graphic Arts
Houghton Library, Harvard University
fMS Typ 195

17) Moses ben Joseph Amarillo (Scribe)
Moses ben Maimon (Moses Maimonides)
Mishneh Torah, 1260
Open to folio 11, floor plan and elevation of the Temple of Jerusalem
From the Felix Friedman Collection.
Presented by a group of donors in 1951.
Houghton Library, Harvard University
Ms. Heb. 36

18) Anonymous Scribe (fifteenth–sixteenth century)
Perez ben Isaac ha-Kohen
Ma'arekhet ha-Elohut
Not illuminated
Presented by a group of donors in 1951
Houghton Library, Harvard University
Ms. Heb. 60

19) Anonymous Craftsman of the Nasrid Kingdom of Granada
Fragment of a Textile, second half of the fourteenth century
Silk and metallic-wrapped silk
40 1/8 x 14 3/4 in.
The Textile Museum
Acquired by George Hewitt Myers in 1931
84.5

ILLUSTRATIONS

Introduction

Fig. 1 Map of Spain, ca. 1400.

Fig. 2 Mudéjar church of San Juan Bautista, Herrera de los Navarros.
Photo courtesy of the author.

Fig. 3 *Retablo mayor* from Santa María, Frómista (Castile).
Photo: Arxiu Mas, Barcelona.

Fig. 4 *Retablo mayor* from San Blas, Anento (Aragon).
Photo: Arxiu Mas, Barcelona.

Fig. 5 *Retablo mayor*, Toledo Cathedral.
Photo: Arxiu Mas, Barcelona.

Fig. 6 Paschal candlestick (Castile).
Photo: © The Metropolitan Museum of Art, New York.

Fig. 7 Tombs of Alvaro de Luna and Juana Pimentel, Luna Chapel, Toledo Cathedral.
Photo: Arxiu Mas, Barcelona.

Fig. 8 Jaume Huguet, *The Coronation of St. Augustine*, Barcelona, Museu d'Art de Catalunya.
Photo: Arxiu Mas, Barcelona.

Catalogue Entries

Fig. 1-1 Bartolomé Bermejo, *St. Engracia.*
Photo by David Bohl.
© Isabella Stewart Gardner Museum, Boston.

Fig. 1-2 Reconstruction of the *Retablo of St. Engracia* (author's reconstruction).
Photo courtesy of the author.

Fig. 1-3 Bartolomé Bermejo, *The Capture of St. Engracia.*
Photo: © San Diego Museum of Art.

Fig. 2-1 Martín Bernat, *St. Blaise Enthroned.*
Photo: © Colnaghi, London and New York.

Fig. 2-2 Bartolomé Bermejo, center panel of the *retablo mayor* of Santo Domingo de Silos, Madrid, Prado.
Photo courtesy of Arxiu Mas, Barcelona.
© Museo del Prado, Madrid.

Fig. 2-3 Martín Bernat, St. *Blaise with Two Deacon Saints*, Lécera, parish church.
Photo: Arxiu Mas, Barcelona.

Fig. 3-1 Francesc Comes, *The Virgin and Child, Sts. George, Martin, and Anthony Abbott.*
Photo by David Bohl.
© Isabella Stewart Gardner Museum, Boston

Fig. 3-2 Francesc Comes, *St. George Killing the Dragon*, Palma de Mallorca, Museo de Mallorca.
Photo: Arxiu Mas, Barcelona.

Fig. 4-1 Pere García de Benabarre, *St. Michael.*
Photo by David Bohl.
© Isabella Stewart Gardner Museum, Boston

Fig. 4-2 Pere García de Benabarre, *St. Jerome*, Barcelona, Museu d'Art de Catalunya.
Photo: Arxiu Mas, Barcelona.

Fig. 4-3 Pere García de Benabarre, *The Feast of Herod*, Barcelona, Museu d'Art de Catalunya.
Photo: Arxiu Mas, Barcelona.

Fig. 5-1 Gonçal Peris de Sarrià, *St. Lucy.*
Photo: © Williams College Museum of Art, Williamstown, Mass.

Fig. 5-2 Gonçal Peris de Sarrià, *Retablo of St. Barbara* from Puertomingalvo, Barcelona, Museu d'Art de Catalunya.
Photo: Arxiu Mas, Barcelona.

Fig. 6-1 Circle of Rodrigo and Francesc de Osona, *Agony in the Garden.*
Photo by Del Bogart.
© Museum of Art, Rhode Island School of Design.

Fig. 6-2 Francesc de Osona, *Epiphany*, London, Victoria and Albert Museum.
Photo: Arxiu Mas, Barcelona.

Fig. 6-3 Paolo da San Leocadio, *Agony in the Garden*, Madrid, Marqués de Montortal Collection.
Photo: Arxiu Mas, Barcelona.

Fig. 7 *Bowl with the Arms of Aragon and Sicily.*
Photo: © The Minneapolis Institute of Arts.

Fig. 8 Anonymous, *Virgin and Child with Female Saint and St. Jerome.*
Photo: © The Metropolitan Museum of Art, New York.

Fig. 9 Master of the Catholic Kings, *The Presentation in the Temple.*
Photo: © President and Fellows, Harvard College, Harvard University Art Museums.

Fig. 9-2 *Retablo mayor*, Avila Cathedral.
Photo: Arxiu Mas, Barcelona.

Fig. 10-1 Pedro Berruguete, *Assumption of the Virgin.*
Photo by David Caras.
© Davis Museum and Cultural Center, Wellesley College,
Gift of Mr. and Mrs. A. M. Adler

Fig. 10-2 Michael Sittow, *Assumption of the Virgin* from the *Polyptych of Queen Isabel*, Washington, D.C., National Gallery of Art, Alba Mellon Bruce Fund.
Photo: © National Gallery of Art, Washington, D.C.

Fig. 10-3 Castilian Master, *Assumption of the Virgin with St. Thomas Receiving the Virgin's Belt* from the *retablo mayor* of Santa María de Arbás, Mayorga (now new parish church).
Photo courtesy of the author.

Fig. 11-1 *Tomb Figure of a Knight.*
Photo: © Isabella Stewart Gardner Museum, Boston.

Fig. 11-2 Tomb of Ruberto de Santisteban, Salamanca, San Martín.
Photo: Arxiu Mas, Barcelona.

Fig. 12 *Royal Arms of the Catholic Kings.*
Photo: © Isabella Stewart Gardner Museum, Boston.

Fig. 13-1 Gil de Siloe, *St. James the Greater.*
Photo: © The Metropolitan Museum of Art, New York; The Cloisters Collection, 1969.

Fig. 13-2 Tomb of King Juan II and Queen Isabel of Portugal, Carthusian Monastery of Miraflores, near Burgos.
Photo: Arxiu Mas, Barcelona.

Fig. 14 Folio 15v, *Donor Portrait*, from *Book of Hours.*
Attributed to the workshop of Juan de Carrión.
Photo by David Loggie.
© Pierpont Morgan Library, New York.
M. 854, f. 15v.

Fig. 15 Folio 1, half-page miniature of two angels holding the arms of Archbishop Carrillo, from St. Augustine's *City of God*. Attributed to Cano de Aranda.
Photo: © The Metropolitan Museum of Art, New York.

Fig. 16 Folio 1, illuminated frontispiece, showing the collection markings of the marquis of Santillana, from *De Regimine Principium*, by Egidio Romano.
Attributed to Jorge Inglés.
Photo: © Harvard College Library, Photographic Services.

Fig. 17 Folio 11, illustrated floor plan and elevation of the Temple of Jerusalem.
Photo: © Harvard College Library, Photographic Services.

Cat. No. 18 Not illustrated.

Fig. 19-1 Nasrid textile fragment.
Photo: © The Textile Museum, Washington, D.C.

This catalogue was designed by Ruth Abrahams and printed by
Mercantile Printing, Inc.
It is set in Minion and Goudy Lombardic.